MARGARET OF ANJOU

MARGARET OF ANJOU

SHE-WOLF OF FRANCE, TWICE QUEEN OF ENGLAND

JOANNA ARMAN

AMBERLEY

To Professor Michael Hicks, who taught me (almost) everything I know about the fifteenth century, and Dr James Ross, who taught me the rest.

Also, to Elena Woodacre who shares my love of Christine de Pizan and my sympathy for Margaret.

First published 2023

Amberley Publishing
The Hill, Stroud
Gloucestershire, GL5 4EP

www.amberley-books.com

Copyright © Joanna Arman, 2023

The right of Joanna Arman to be identified as the Author of this work has been asserted in accordance with the Copyright, Designs and Patents Act 1988.

ISBN 978 1 4456 8358 4 (hardback)
ISBN 978 1 4456 8359 1 (ebook)

British Library Cataloguing in Publication Data.
A catalogue record for this book is available from the British Library.

1 2 3 4 5 6 7 8 9 10

Typesetting by SJmagic DESIGN SERVICES, India.
Printed in the UK.

CONTENTS

PROLOGUE

She was a descendant of Eleanor of Aquitaine, and the last foreign-born queen of medieval England. Chroniclers called her unnatural and perverse; over a century after her death Shakespeare dubbed her 'the she-wolf of France', with a 'tiger's heart wrapped in a woman's hide'. He didn't mean it as a compliment.

Margaret of Anjou. Her name still stirs up strong feelings today. Indeed, I argue that after Richard III she is probably one of the most controversial and maligned figures of the period known as the Wars of the Roses. Margaret's defenders argue that she was a strong and courageous woman dealt a bad hand, who tried but ultimately failed to make it in a man's world; that she was defamed and vilified by contemporaries suspicious of foreigners and fearful of female power. Her detractors argue that she was a medieval *femme fatale*: the real-life inspiration for Cersei Lannister. A cruel, manipulative, and power-hungry tyrant who hated her adoptive country, oppressed and killed its people and tried to place her illegitimate offspring on the throne.

In this new biography, I aim to strip away the layers of myth and propaganda to find the real Margaret of Anjou. To do this, it is necessary to look beyond the almost two decades of her life in which she was embroiled in the political and dynastic struggles known to history as the Wars of the Roses. There was so much more to this remarkable woman, whose eventful life spanned five decades of the medieval period's final century.

She was born to the scion of an ancient French dynasty. When she was little more than a year old, Joan of Arc was burned at the stake. During her childhood, her father became a prisoner of war and she was raised in the household of her Spanish grandmother, who had been an early patron of Joan. Her father called himself the King of Jerusalem, and her brother became a renowned crusader.

Her lifetime saw the introduction of the printing press to Europe, and the first printed books in the English language. In her twenty-third year the great city of Constantinople fell to the Turks, more than a millennium after it was established. A few months later, the Hundred Years War ended in victory for her homeland. In Italy, the Renaissance was in full swing. Nicolo Machiavelli, Thomas More and Erasmus were all born in her lifetime.

She established a college in an internationally renowned educational institution which still exists to this day. Her husband founded a college and a school. She was a patron of learning, scholarship and invention. One of her closest friends bore the name of a famous English poet; another, said to be a witch, became mother-in-law to Margaret's deadliest enemy. She was the aunt and cousin of the first Tudor king, but she would not live to see him crowned.

This is her story.

I

A CHILD OF LITTLE ACCOUNT

Margaret was born on 23 March 1430 in the small town of Pont-à-Mousson in the county of Lorraine in eastern France. This is virtually all that is known about the circumstances of her birth. When it comes to kings and princes, many more details are available: the building in which they were born, the exact time of day. Margaret of Anjou, however, was neither queen nor heir to a royal throne.

Her father was René, Duke of Anjou, and her mother was René's first wife Isabelle of Lorraine. Margaret was the fifth of ten children from their marriage, although only three would survive into adulthood. René and Isabelle had two sons and a daughter living at the time of her birth, so it may be said that Margaret was a child of little account: the youngest daughter of a French noble family, albeit one with royal connections. They could not have known that this little French girl would go on to play a seminal and sometimes controversial role in the history of France's belligerent northern neighbour.

Margaret was a popular name throughout Europe in the later Middle Ages. Hundreds can be found in various records and sources from the period. As with most of the first names in medieval Europe, Margaret was a saint's name, though its historical origin is obscure. The antecedent was probably Margaret of Antioch, one of many virgin martyrs believed to have lived in ancient times and been tortured to death for her refusal to renounce Christianity and marry a pagan. Her feast day fell on 26 (or maybe 13) July, so it seems unlikely that René chose the name because her birth coincided with the saint's day. Incidentally, St Margaret was supposed to take a special interest in women in labour, often being invoked for a safe delivery. Many years later, Margaret of Anjou may have sought the saint's intercession herself.[1]

Margaret's mother gave birth to her brood of ten over thirteen years, so there wasn't a large age gap between Margaret and her siblings. Her sister Yolande (possibly one of twins) was about eighteen months her senior and was named after the girls' famous grandmother, Yolande of Aragon. Margaret surely have had a normal childhood by the standards of the fifteenth-century nobility. She would have spent the first seven or so years of her life in her family's household and in the care of nurses and maids and other women, probably seeing little of her mother, let alone her father. A 'household' in the context of the medieval European aristocracy included not only family members but also servants, retainers and other people such as wards or knights. It encompassed anyone who lived with and worked for them.

Margaret would have had a normal education for a fifteenth-century noble child. Contrary to popular opinion, there is no specific evidence that certain subjects were considered unsuitable or forbidden for women. We tend to think of the Renaissance as something that happened in the sixteenth century, but it technically started in the fourteenth. By the time of Margaret's birth in 1430, the European Renaissance was in full swing, and this would have had an impact on her education. One of the characteristics of Renaissance education was great emphasis on the works of classical Greek and Roman authors. These works were not simply a form of entertainment but were also considered to be morally and politically instructive.

One of the authors possibly familiar to Margaret was Christine de Pisan, who was in fact a close contemporary and countrywoman of hers. Christine held very strong views on women's roles in society and their behaviour. She railed against the sexist attitudes prevailing in her day, including the notion that women were less intelligent and less capable than men, and unsuited to hold powerful positions in government.

Before her death, Christine is known to have been an ardent supporter of Joan of Arc and took no issue with her donning armour or taking part in combat. One wonders what her view of Margaret would have been during the Wars of the Roses. Perhaps she would have been sympathetic to one of her countrywomen fighting to defend her family. That said, although she advocated that some noblewomen including baronesses should learn how to use weapons if necessary to defend their lands and people, Christine's views on the model behaviour of women higher up the social scale was rather more conservative. Her model princess was kind, gentle, patient, humble and above all obedient. Such virtues did not really lend themselves well to the situation Margaret would have to face before she had turned thirty.

Leaving this aside, it seems likely that Margaret would have been exposed to Christine de Pisan's works in some way; after all, they were medieval bestsellers. She drew many examples from classical mythology and literature, more or less inevitable for any author at the time. Heroines from the Trojan War, the legendary Amazons, Cassandra, Julius Caesar's daughter Julia, and Dido, founder of Carthage, all feature in her *Le Livre de la Cité des Dames* (*The Book of the City of Ladies*), which was finished in 1405. Chivalric romances were also popular. We know that Margaret's grandmother Yolande of Aragon favoured the romance of Mélusine, a fanciful tale about a water fairy who took human form. The story usually involves her marrying a French nobleman sometimes identified as Guy of Lusignan, Count of Poitou, who later became the King of Jerusalem, or in some cases his near contemporary Raymond of Poitou. After using magical arts to build a castle and having several children, Mélusine's true nature is revealed and she flies away, never to be seen again. Yolande and various other

French nobles claimed descent from the mythical fairy woman. Incidentally, so too did Jacquetta of Luxembourg, wife of John, Duke of Bedford and later the mother of Elizabeth Woodville. An earlier version of the story involved the predecessors of the Plantagenet kings through their common ancestor Geoffrey of Anjou. Richard the Lionheart was allegedly fond of the tale and used to enjoy claiming descent from a demon. Margaret was actually sprung from the same Angevin line and had an interesting connection with the family's origin myth.

It is likely that Margaret learned English early on, if not before her marriage then only shortly afterwards. One gently amusing scene in Shakespeare's *Henry V* sees the titular king attempt to chat up Katherine de Valois in broken French because his bride cannot understand English, but this is fiction. Henry spoke French fluently. Most if not all English nobles mastered the language of their continental neighbours, and for nearly three centuries after the Norman Conquest it had been the official language at court. People from the two countries interacted so frequently that knowing one another's language was necessary. If all else failed, one could even communicate in Latin.

Margaret's father René of Anjou was something of a Renaissance prince. He was known to have taken more than a passing interest in the kind of literature that influenced the aforementioned Christine de Pizan, and in his later years he actually wrote a number of books. There is a tendency to assume that Margaret's father was a relatively unimportant French nobleman, and many are unaware of her ancestral connections to the Plantagenet dynasty that she would later marry into. Duke René was a descendant in the ancient line of the counts of Anjou, the same line from whence the Plantagenet kings of England had sprung three centuries before. Margaret was in fact descended from the Plantagenets twice over, through both her father and her paternal grandmother, the formidable Yolande of Aragon.

Yolande was the kingmaker of fifteenth-century France. In 1425 she arranged for the former Dauphin, Charles, to marry her daughter. This event may not seem especially significant – on the face of it a typical medieval dynastic marriage – but it proved to be crucial to Charles and the Kingdom of France as a whole. Charles was the youngest surviving son of King Charles IV of France and Isabeau of Bavaria. In the natural order of things, he should have automatically succeeded his father as King of France. He did not. The reason was Henry V, King of England. Under the terms of the Treaty of Troyes, Henry was named as King Charles's successor. The treaty was of course the crowning glory of Henry's conquest of France, the result of several military campaigns spanning five years. Despite some modern reinterpretations of his personality and reputation, Henry achieved more in that five years than his ancestors had in two decades. Edward III, his great-grandfather, had fought in France and won two famous battles. He had even captured the King of France and his son, but he had never been named as the successor.

By the terms of the Treaty of Troyes, Henry was betrothed to Katherine de Valois. (Interestingly, the later marriage of Katherine's younger brother to Yolande of Aragon's daughter would actually make Katherine an aunt by marriage of Margaret of Anjou, although the two never met.) Charles had not always been Dauphin, and he was not the notorious son of the French king who appeared in Shakespeare's *Henry V*; that was his older brother, Louis, who died in 1416.

Alongside her political manoeuvres in support of the French, Yolande was also one of the earliest and most important patrons of Joan of Arc. Much has been written on Joan over the years and this book is not about her, but the events that were concurrent with Margaret's early life are relevant. It is believed that Yolande was the woman who orchestrated Joan's famous meeting with Charles in 1429 when she recognised the king among a crowd of his courtiers, even when he was wearing a disguise. Joan's recognition of Charles may have been less due to divine inspiration and more to do with having been coached or prompted by contacts in the royal court.

Joan, of course, is often credited with having made it possible for Charles to be crowned in Rouen in defiance of Henry's rule. She cleared the path through enemy territory to allow him to get to the ancient and sacred place where French kings were crowned. Yet, it has been argued that she could not have done it without Yolande. Margaret's grandmother was constantly working behind the scenes, raising Joan's profile, sourcing contacts and providing the springboard for the role she played on the political stage. One cannot help but wonder whether Joan was really

Yolande's handmaiden as much as God's. The mighty lady felt the need to give the Almighty a helping hand.

Yolande's role in the rise of Joan of Arc shows something of her propensity for intriguing and politicking. She was working against the English and in favour of her husband's homeland almost from the outset. It's easy to underestimate the pivotal role that women played in medieval politics, especially if they were from outside the royal family. Yolande seems to have been an especially astute woman, using her familial connections to her advantage and, as she saw it, the greater advantage of France.

By March 1430, Joan's career was also at its zenith. In August of the previous year she had led the force which relieved the Siege of Orleans, but for several months a truce with the English had left her kicking her proverbial heels in Paris. In March 1430 she dictated (all of Joan's correspondence was dictated as she herself was illiterate) a letter to the Hussites of Bohemia. The Hussites were a group deemed heretical by the fifteenth-century church, taking their name from the priest Jan Hus, who had been condemned as a heretic and burned in 1415. It has been suggested that Huss himself was influenced by the writings and teachings of the fourteenth-century English cleric and theologian John Wycliffe. There is no direct evidence for this, but there were certainly some parallels in their teachings and the ideas espoused by the movements they inspired, among them a strong emphasis on reading the scriptures in the vernacular and taking a stand against corruption within the church. The Hussites were far more successful but also more militant than the English Lollards, and Bohemia ended up plunging into full-scale religious war between Hussite lords and forces loyal to the mainstream church.

Joan, despite her saintly reputation today, was imbued with the enthusiastic zeal of a crusader. In the fifteenth century, the two were far from mutually exclusive. Her letter to the recalcitrant Hussites threatened to wipe them out if they did not give up their heretical beliefs willingly. Some sources date the composition of this letter to 23 March 1430 – the very same day as Margaret's birth. Two months later to the day, Joan was captured in the rearguard of a French force as they were retreating to Compiègne following an unsuccessful attempt to attack a Burgundian encampment.

The events of Joan's trial and execution the following year are well documented, but it is notable that neither Charles VII nor indeed Yolande of Aragon used their influence to try to help her. It is true that she had ceased to be politically useful for some time before, but it was not simple fear of the English (as some writers claimed) that stopped them. Few could afford to be seen to support a person even accused of heresy, let alone a person convicted of it. Charles VII's reputation was already tarnished and his position precarious enough in 1431 without earning the animosity of the church by siding with a woman believed to be a heretic, if not a witch. So, on 30 May 1431, when Margaret would have been approximately fourteen months old, Joan of Arc was burned at the stake.

In 1430, another event that would later prove important to Margaret's life was taking place. On 23 April (which just happened to be St George's Day), her future husband, Henry VI, had landed in Calais on what became known as his 'coronation expedition'. On 16 December the following year, Henry was crowned King of France in the cathedral of Notre-Dame in Paris. That it took over eighteen months from the time Henry landed for him to be crowned testifies to Joan of Arc's lasting effect on French morale. Even if we doubt her actual capacity as a commander or military leader, in enabling the son of King Charles VI and Isabeau of Bavaria to be crowned King of France she reinforced and invigorated the French war effort.

Before 1430, Dauphin Charles had not been a credible contender for the throne – at least not according to the English, anyway. Despite being the youngest and only surviving son of Charles VI, his involvement in the murder of Charles the Bold, Duke of Burgundy back in 1418 had done much to discredit him. Although he had only been a teenager at the time of the fateful event, and the extent of his involvement is debated, the murder of the famous nobleman destroyed any chances of reconciliation between France and Burgundy, which had been at loggerheads since the opening years of the fifteenth century. Since the Burgundians had long since been allies of the English, it also played right into their hands. By the time of the Treaty of Troyes in 1420, the English were able to depict the Dauphin as a murderer and traitor. Not only did he lack moral credibility to be a ruler, but there were also rumours of him being illegitimate. Following his father's death in October 1422, he spent most of his time in the Loire Valley, even establishing an unofficial court there.

However, the English had retained control of most of northern France for the eight years following Henry V's death, including Paris, where French kings were traditionally crowned. Although Charles made repeated and valiant attempts to dislodge them, all of these proved unsuccessful and for the remainder of the 1420s the English remained largely unassailable. During this time Charles earned the derogatory epithet of 'King of Bourges', after a town in the Loire Valley because his court-in-exile was based there, and because of his close association with the House of Anjou.

Charles's fortuitous (or arranged) meeting with Joan of Arc, and his coronation at Rouen in 1429, provided his rule with the sacral blessing and legitimacy that he so desperately needed. Of course, there had always been die-hard supporters of the Valois dynasty who had supported him and refused to accept Henry as France's rightful ruler, but events since 1418 had knocked Charles's confidence as well as his reputation. Though the death of Joan in 1431 later proved to be a setback, and the French were in a weak position in the opening years of the 1430s, Yolande of Aragon was arguably at the height of her power and influence. Her daughter was married to the King of France, a man whose association with Joan would later be vindicated at her retrial. Yolande's sons were a rather different matter.

Parents

Margaret of Anjou's parents, René of Anjou and Isabelle of Lorraine, are worthy of note. Duke René of Anjou was the son of Yolande. He held or laid claim to an impressive range of titles in his lifetime; he was not only Duke of Anjou by inheritance, but also added to his titles Count of Provence, Duke of Bar, Duke of Lorraine and Count of Piedmont. He acquired Lorraine through his marriage to Isabella, heiress of Charles, Duke of Lorraine, and the Duchy of Bar by right of his mother. He wasn't even supposed to be Duke of Anjou, only coming to that title when his older brother Louis died without heirs in 1435, by which time Margaret would have been about five years old.

English writers today tend to regard René as a relatively minor French nobleman with pretensions of grandeur, because alongside his other titles he was also called King of Naples and King of Jerusalem. The former title harked back the Norman conquest of Sicily in the eleventh century and the latter had been held by the leaders of the Crusader states. In calling himself a king, was René merely trying to enhance his status? Perhaps not. His claim to the title of King of Naples, at least, was based on his relationship to Joanna II, Queen of Naples.

It's also common to emphasise that René was relatively poor, and his land had limited resources. This actually wasn't his fault. What impoverished the Duchy of Anjou was a long dispute over the Duchy of Lorraine between René and his wife's cousin Antoine de Voudemont. Antoine was the nephew of Charles, Duke of Lorraine and considered himself to be the rightful heir of his uncle, who only had daughters. After Charles's death in 1431, Antoine went to war with René over his claim, and took him hostage at the Battle of Bulgnéville in July of that year. It was René's 'long and expensive' period of captivity which left the Duchy of Anjou in dire financial straits as his family had to raise money to pay for his ransom and endure long years of diplomatic wrangling not just to bring about his release but to resolve the dispute. Ultimately, the Holy Roman Emperor was to decide that René was the rightful heir, but it took several years and two betrothals.[2]

René was taken captive when Margaret was about five years old. From captivity he 'bestowed full executive and military authority' upon his wife, Isabelle, who sent Margaret to Yolande's household while she busied herself dealing with the family's lands in Italy. Margaret remained with Yolande until her death in 1442.[3] It was not the first time the erstwhile Duchess of Anjou had played host to relatives or to other nobles; Charles VII had lived with Yolande for several years during his adolescence. In fact, it has been argued that Charles came to view her as a mother figure because he had so little to do with his biological mother, Isabeau of Bavaria.

Years later, Yolande took in her daughter-in-law and her youngest children while she negotiated for the release of her son. This makes it seem that Margaret stayed with her grandmother twice in her life: once in her infancy, during her father's first spell as a prisoner of war, and then after 1439. It was quite possible for a person to communicate with others when technically a 'prisoner', so there need not be any contradiction here, as it appears René wrote to his wife while captive. The main problem is one of a conflation of dates. Some sources say that Margaret lived with her mother until she was nine or ten, others that she was sent to her grandmother at a young age.

At the age of eight or nine, Yolande sent for her granddaughter to come and stay with her. Her family had been residing in Italy at the time (René did claim to be King of Naples after all), and it was probably the girl's first time away from them. Margaret's grandmother seems to have taken a special interest in her youngest surviving granddaughter, to the point of requesting she come from Italy to live in her household. This was consistent with her history of providing and fighting for her family members, and also with her desire to extend her personal and political influence. It has been said that Margaret lived with her grandmother until the age of fifteen, shortly before her marriage. However, this is likely a mistake by later historians since Yolande died in November 1442, when Margaret would have been twelve.

It is natural to assume that Margaret's childhood experiences were formative. Her father was absent for much of her early life, and she was effectively raised by her mother and grandmother. Isabel and especially Yolande both provided her with examples of women who could wield power effectively in the absence of a man. Not that this was a situation either woman chose; it was forced upon them by circumstances.

One other aspect of her grandmother's legacy that may have made an impression on young Margaret was how assertively and determinedly she fought for her family and for their interests, whether behind the scenes or openly. An allegation levelled at Margaret today is that she acted against the interests of England because she was French. Yet her grandmother was Spanish by birth, and that had not stopped her from loyally serving the French royal family and the interests of France, having married a Frenchman.

Even as her father's youngest child, and a girl, Margaret would not have been denied an education. In fact, her father was so enamoured of art and literature that his Angevin court became known as a cultural centre. This did not happen until after his mother's death, however, by which time Margaret would have been approaching her teens.

Duke René's interest in the arts went far beyond what was normal for a fifteenth-century nobleman. He wrote three (possibly four) books, including a work of allegory, a work of religious devotion called *The Mortification of Vain Pleasure* and a romance about a love quest entitled *The Book of the Love-Smitten Heart*. He also penned a short treatise about tournaments, *Le Livre de Tournois*, recording rules and correct conduct. He is also known to have been an amateur painter, and various works of art are wrongly attributed to him today. Some Ricardians now use the Yorkist king's interest in music, books and architecture as evidence that he would have ushered the Renaissance into England, but it was already here. Even if the claims about Richard were true, Margaret of Anjou's father far outstripped him in his cultural pursuits.

Trouble in France

The year 1435 was not only propitious for Margaret's family but for whole of France and England. In September, John, Duke of Bedford, younger brother of King Henry V and Regent of France, died following a short illness. Bedford had proved a capable and respected leader in France for over a decade, working tirelessly to preserve his brother's conquests in France and to protect his nephew's legacy. He did not live to witness a final and bitter act of betrayal (as he saw it) when the Duke of Burgundy agreed to a treaty with his long-term enemies and was finally reconciled with King Charles. This agreement, known as the Treaty of Arras, practically marked the end of the Anglo-Burgundian alliance that had been so important to the English war effort. It was ratified on 21 September 1435; Duke John had died just a week earlier.

The treaty resulted from a prolonged conference, which had been convened as a means of coming to some sort of negotiated settlement and perhaps ending the war. On 6 September the English envoys broke off negotiations and left. The Duke of Burgundy's final accord and reconciliation with the King of France was a hard lesson for Henry VI; indeed, it was one of the only times in his career when he actually expressed anger. Although Henry wanted peace, he took Burgundy's abandonment of their decades-long alliance, which had been so crucial to English success in

France, as a personal betrayal. From this point on, the war with France reads as a round of disasters for England.

Later in the 1430s, the veteran general John Talbot was sent back to France with various lieutenants under him including Richard, Duke York. He succeeded in regaining and holding some territory for several years, but the French eventually won it back and began to regain more territory, especially after the release of nobles like the Duke of Orleans. As the war progressed, Henry increasingly showed his inclination to make peace – almost to a fault at times, given his uncle the Duke of Gloucester and other nobles seem to have been in favour of continuing the conflict indefinitely. It was negotiations for peace that prompted discussions of a French match for King Henry. The English had been putting out feelers for a possible French wife for the king as early as 1439, but at that time full recognition of Henry VI's sovereignty over France was a condition, affirming what his father had achieved.

By the early years of the following decade, when Margaret was approaching her teens, she had already had more than one suitor. One of the most illustrious was the Holy Roman Emperor himself, said to have been attracted by tales of Margaret's beauty. It was normal for high-born ladies to be praised for their fairness, but Margaret's appearance was already described in glowing terms at the tender age of twelve. The match with the emperor ultimately fell through, probably due to Yolande's death in 1442 and René's continued absence.

By the following year, René was back and entertaining another proposal for his daughter's hand. This time her prospective suitor was the Duke of Burgundy's nephew Charles, Duke of Nevers. The arrangement between the duke and the head of a family who had been implacably opposed to the English throughout the war reveals something about how alliances had changed in the years after the Treaty of Arras. Interestingly, Duke René agreed to settle a dowry of 50,000 livres on his daughter. This match also failed to come to anything, this time for political reasons. The duke's long-term opponent and rival Antoine Vaudemont went to King Charles and expressed disapproval of the proposed marriage, and so negotiations were postponed and eventually dropped.[4]

As 1444 began, Margaret was living at the French court. Another source was soon singing her praises; a Burgundian chronicler by the name of Barante wrote, 'There was no princess in Christendom more accomplished than my Lady Margaret. She is already renowned in France for her beauty and wit and her lofty spirit of courage.'[5] She was popular at court and enjoyed taking part in traditional entertainments and activities; she even had a champion carrying her colours in jousts (see page 131).

It was in this year that the King of England started to pay attention to Margaret. His choice would prove controversial among his subjects for a number of reasons, not least that she came without a substantial dowry. It is hard to discern quite why this was, since her father had been willing to offer one for her first suitor; perhaps René pleaded poverty in a subtle but intentional snub to the English, whom he 'ran rings around' during the negotiations. On the other hand, the feud with his cousin and his periods of imprisonment would have been costly, as was his renewed engagement in the war with England.

What was to prove most controversial about the match with Margaret, though, was that at some point during negotiations the English ambassadors agreed to give up the county of Maine as part of the marriage contract. Later chroniclers would be horrified by this action, remarking that not only had Margaret come without a dowry, but the King had had to pay for her: 'The Englishmen told me that the King of England took her without any dowry, and even restored some lands which he held to her father,' wrote the baffled Milanese Raffaelo De Negra to the Duchess of Milan more than a decade later.

The reality was actually far more complicated. The ceding of Maine was actually part of a series of long-term negotiations to bring about a peaceful conclusion to the war in France. The French were adamant that Henry had to give up his claims to its throne, but his ambassadors were fighting to retain his rights to certain ancestral lands. Henry's marriage to Margaret brought about a much-needed two-year truce in hostilities. At the same time, it was hoped that the French king could take a more 'sympathetic direction' towards the English retaining certain other lands, especially Normandy. It was give and take, not just a simple matter of the English giving up one parcel of land with nothing to show for it.[6]

Henry was formally betrothed to Margaret on 21 June 1444, but she did not arrive in England for their marriage until nearly a year later. It wasn't that unusual for there to be a relatively long gap between betrothal and marriage (sometimes a period of years elapsed). Of course, the diplomatic negotiations went on for the whole of that period, but Margaret herself seems to have suffered badly in the lead-up to her departure for England. Indeed, she reportedly burst into tears when she was separated from her uncle King Charles in March 1445.[7] This was followed by complaints of severe stomach pains, for which there are records of expensive physicians' bills.

It's difficult to diagnose illness from a distance of more than 500 years, but some recent historians have suggested she may have been suffering from stress, or some kind of anxiety severe enough to keep her from setting off for several weeks. We know today that anxiety can indeed result in illness or debilitating physical symptoms, and Margaret had good cause to be anxious. She had only just turned fifteen and was expected to leave her homeland for a country whose rulers had been her sworn enemy for most of her life. Even if Henry was a good man, she didn't know anyone in England, and had probably only met a few English people in France such as the Duke of Suffolk. She must have been nervous, frightened and uncertain about her future.

2

A ROYAL MARRIAGE

Henry had to send fifty-six ships to transport Margaret and her entourage to England, and a large retinue to escort her to the wedding at Titchfield Abbey in Hampshire,[1] but the couple were finally wed on 23 April 1445, Saint George's day. Margaret had already apparently been married to Henry by proxy at Tours in France some months before, with the Duke of Suffolk standing in for the groom. (Contrary to what Shakespeare would imply in his later play, there is no evidence Suffolk wanted to marry Margaret himself.) It is possible that they were married in the relatively nondescript location of Titchfield as a result of her continued illness, or because Henry just wanted to make sure the marriage took place as soon as possible.

Controversy surrounded Henry and Margaret's marriage from the beginning. Why didn't King Charles VII of France offer Henry one of his own daughters in marriage? After all, two of his sisters had been married to English kings. It is possible that he wanted to avoid creating too close a familial connection with the kings of England, who had of course directly laid claim to the throne of France before, usually by right of their marriages to French princesses. There was also the fact that Charles's children happened to be first cousins of King Henry, but that had never been an insurmountable obstacle to royal matches in the past.

In the end, both parties had decided that the youngest daughter of René of Anjou was the best option. The English favoured the Angevin match in the hopes that her family, whose lands bordered Normandy, might help them in protecting the region. This may seem like a foolish idea, especially considering the anti-English stance of the Duke of Anjou, but it made sense; if his daughter were married to the King of England, the English would leave his lands well alone, and he was more likely to honour any agreement made between the French and the English crown by being connected to both.

Above all, it was known that Charles's court was riven with factions, and being allied with the head of the most powerful one through marriage might allow the English to hammer out favourable terms in the treaty of which this marriage formed a part.

Years after the wedding, hostile chroniclers and writers would suggest that Henry was essentially duped into marrying Margaret by the French through foils such as the Duke of Suffolk. Such claims were retrospective and usually written after Henry's initial downfall, or in the turbulent later years of his reign. At the time, Suffolk was applauded as a hero for his role in securing the terms of the Treaty of Tours, 'receiving handsome thanks from the commons and a commendation from [the Duke of] Gloucester and the rest of the Lords'.[2]

Contemporary sources almost universally speak well of Margaret, especially when she entered London for her coronation:

> As she came through the city, many devices were displayed and stories told, with angels and other heavenly figures, and songs and melodies heard in several places. The conduits ran with wine, both white and red, for all the people who wished to drink ... On the morrow, which was Sunday, the coronation and feast were royally and worthily held at Westminster in the king's palace.[3]

So remarked the author of the *Brut*, a chronicle that recorded major events in England over many years. No expense was spared on pageants or partying to celebrate the arrival of the new teenage queen that summer. The same source refers to Margaret wearing a coronel studded with pearls and precious stones and being escorted by forty-six knights whose horses were decorated with damask threaded with gold.

Nor is there any need to assume that the happiness and excitement was contrived or false. It's true that the treasury basically paid for the celebrations, but the people of England may well have been excited and elated at the prospect of a new queen. There had not been one for a quarter of a century, after all, since Henry V's brief marriage to Katherine de Valois in 1420, and so Margaret was an 'emblem and the promise of a hopeful future'. Most other observers praised Margaret for her virtues and her beauty, as the model princess and queen at the time of her coronation. Vergil would later praise her as 'exceeding ... in wisdom, imbued with courage above the nature of her sex, her noble acts manifestly declared'.[4]

There is no hint of hostility towards her at this time, and the people of England seem to have fully accepted their new queen in the summer of 1445. For the first eight years of her reign, Margaret seems to have largely fulfilled the roles that were expected of her, and not stood out very much. These roles included providing good lordship (or ladyship) and being an intercessor between the people and her husband, although with Henry VI it would not seem that such a role was necessary. The 'intercessory' role, however, could be more legal and theoretical than literal. Not all queens had to kneel before their husbands to prevent them from hanging the burghers of Calais.

The matter of Maine soon came back to haunt Margaret and the English government, when the county was finally handed over to the French in 1447. That it took two full years from the time of Henry's marriage until the county was handed back is interesting. People must have known that this was one of the terms of the agreement made in 1444, and yet later observers would remark on the event as an unexpected and sudden act of treachery which the

English surely would never have sanctioned. Perhaps they expected that Maine would be kept by somehow wriggling out of the agreement.

Margaret made connections with some English nobles before she set foot on English soil. One of the most notable was of course William de la Pole, Duke of Suffolk, who had stood in for the groom when she had been married to Henry by proxy. She also soon met his wife Alice de la Pole (*neé* Chaucer, granddaughter of the famous poet of the same name), and the two became lifelong friends. Another was John Talbot, Earl of Shrewsbury, a seasoned commander who incidentally did not favour peace with France; the fact that she was able to befriend a man who could be expected to feel antipathy for her demonstrates that she was prepared to see past political animosity when it came to personal relationships.

At her wedding Talbot gifted Margaret a Book of Hours, a type of devotional work that was popular in later medieval Europe. These books contained prayers and extracts from the Psalms and other Bible texts which corresponded to daily services held in monasteries. They were often richly illustrated and incorporated more secular material reflecting the interests of the owner or the commissioner. In Margaret's case, the Book of Hours given to her by Talbot contained poetry as well as extracts from romances and political works. It also contained an illustration of Margaret's marriage to Henry, which is one of the most famous depictions of her. It shows the new couple seated, with Henry on the left and Margaret on the right. The royal figures hold hands while gripping sceptres, symbols of their royal status and authority. At the bottom of the image a male figure, probably Talbot himself, is shown kneeling and presenting a book to the queen. Such illustrations were normally found in the front of books, the equivalent of a modern dedication or *ex libris*.

In 1446 or 1447, Margaret petitioned Henry to establish a college. She was imitating her husband, who had established King's College, Cambridge in 1441 and Eton in 1440. The text of the request contains a line saying she wanted to establish the foundation for 'the laud and honour of the sex feminine' among other reasons. Her foundation would become Queen's College, Cambridge. She seems to have visited the site at least twice, in 1446 and 1447. Sir John Wenlock reportedly laid the foundation stone, and 'the college's statutes were formulated with the assistance of William Booth', her chancellor. The foundation and her reasons for wanting to establish the college suggest she was doing more than just aping her husband, and was consciously interested in education and learning, as well as promoting the virtues of the female gender.[5]

Despite her sizable wedding entourage, Margaret had kept a very small retinue and famously arrived without a proper dowry. Most of her servants and retainers were therefore employees, and Henry had to make provision for her to pay them. She was given a dower of 10,000 marks per year in 1446, and later given lands worth £2,000 out of the Duchy of Lancaster and mostly concentrated in the Midlands around Tutbury, Leicester and Kenilworth. These lands had been part of the traditional dowry settlements of fourteenth-century queens, so the king was not doing anything out of the ordinary by granting them to her.[6]

Margaret was also given the custody of one of the kingdom's most valuable heiresses in Anne, daughter of Henry Beauchamp, Earl of Warwick. The purpose of giving a man or woman the custody of a person in royal wardship was to allow that person to profit from the ward's marriage, whether by arranging it themselves or by selling it on. They were also supposed to be able to derive an income from the heir's lands (depending on the nature of the grant) until the heir came of age. The heir would go to live with the guardian, at which point the guardian could also claim funds to 'maintain' the heir in their household. It was for these reasons that the exchange of wardships was such a profitable and lucrative business among the medieval aristocracy. Within a few months Margaret sold Anne's wardship to the Duke of Suffolk, but she made sure to draw some profit from the arrangement beforehand.

In 1447, Margaret was given a grant of money from lands which had been held by Humphrey, Duke of Gloucester, who had recently died while under arrest for treason. This could not have gone down well, as it looked like the throne was profiting from Humphrey's demise, even though seizing the assets of a person accused of treason was quite normal. She also obtained his manor house at Greenwich, which became her favourite residence. In addition to this, she engaged in other money-making schemes such as securing a grant to override a monopoly on the sale of wool.[7] While some would interpret Margaret's behaviour as greedy or acquisitive, it is worth nothing that annuities were not always paid, especially if the funds simply were not available. Medieval English monarchs did not have unlimited amounts of money at their disposal, and sometimes they had to be creative to fund their expenditures. As a child, Margaret had known what relative poverty was like; her father's ransom had left her parents impoverished, and her grandmother Yolande had to manage her own finances carefully. This may have given her a greater appreciation for the value of money, or at least an understanding of what it was like to be in dire financial states – and a corresponding desire to never go back to that.

Surviving correspondence shows Margaret acting as a good lady to her servants and as an intercessory. Most of her remaining letters concern mundane things such as complaints about poaching or trespassing, but we can also see evidence of Margaret working on behalf of people associated with her. Among them were William Boothe, Bishop of Lichfield, who was her personal chancellor.[8] She also employed a chamberlain, Sir John Wenlock, Edward Ellesmere, who had the title of 'clerk of jewels', and a lawyer by the name of Robert Tanfield, who became her attorney general (and later replaced Wenlock as her chamberlain).[9] Since Margaret had come to England with only a small retinue, she took all of these men into her service after her arrival. Wenlock proved to be a controversial figure; by 1453 he had been expelled from Margaret's household on the grounds that he was biased towards the Duke of York, although this didn't stop him being appointed ambassador to France in the later part of the decade. The plot thickened when he was suspected of being a double agent working with the Burgundians to undermine negotiations with France.[10]

A letter from Margaret to William Boothe refers to one John Banham who had been allowed to cut down ten oak trees for timber in the royal estate at Kenilworth. She wrote it to make clear that Banham had permission to fell the trees, which otherwise could have got him into a great deal of trouble. Margaret thus ordered Boothe to deliver a 'warrant' to the keeper of the lands, the fifteenth-century equivalent of a park ranger.[11] This letter, although the subject is fairly straightforward, does showcase an open-handed generosity that rulers were expected to extend towards commoners as well as nobles. Overspending and excessive generosity came to be frequent problems in Henry's reign and were blamed for the king's financial difficulties, although this was an oversimplification.

More serious interventions on Margaret's part included her missive to Nicholas Strange of Islington demanding that he stop preventing his daughter from marrying her servant T. Bugdon, who had contracted a union with her. There was no legal reason for the marriage not to take place, and presumably Katherine had made the contract of her own free will. This is one of the few letters in which it is implied that the wronged party had approached the queen directly to ask her for her intervention. In another such case a London draper said that he had been unjustly deprived of lands.[12] We don't know the queen's relationship to the mysterious T. Bugden, but we do know how she became involved in the case of the draper, whose name was Ralph Josselyn: Ralph's cousin, one Thomas Sharnborne, informed her of the matter.

In both cases the queen was acting as overlord by trying to resolve matters on their behalf. One could ask why they did not go to the king; perhaps he was not available at the time, and the queen was the highest authority available. In Ralph Josselyn's case, his cousin was also referred to as 'our squire', so was presumably a squire in the household of Margaret herself. A number of the members of Margaret's household had also been in the king's service at some point, and they even shared some of their personnel at times. There was no real difficulty in this since the king and queen were hardly ever apart in the first five years of their marriage.[13]

Going to the top to get grievances redressed was the main aim for petitioners; the particular royal they reached was less of a consideration. We do not know of any specific evidence that queens received or heard petitions as kings did, but it is quite possible. Margaret had her own council which oversaw all matters relating to the administration of her dower lands in the Duchy of Lancaster, and it also had judicial and advisory functions. They met each day and even had a special room assigned to them in the palace of Westminster. If the queen ever received petitions, it is likely that she heard them there, or that they were presented to one of her councillors.

In this case, the petitioners would have tried to see the queen or one of her close retainers who could bring the matter before her. Josselyn had the good fortune of having a relative associated with the royal household and so could ask his cousin to have a word with the queen when he was next at court. Since both were based in London, this probably happened during one of the periods when she was staying in or near the capital. For the most part, however, Margaret's council served to pursue her interests and oversee the day-to-day running of her estates. She employed several lawyers to represent her in cases before the Chancery and the court of Common Pleas. These would not have been major criminal cases; most concerned land, property or financial affairs.

While Margaret could act on behalf of others and could get involved through her representatives in legal cases, she could not take a visible political role. Removed from the inner workings of court, she likely had no inkling of the trouble that was brewing.

By this time, the divisions and factions in Henry's court were becoming ever more noticeable. They had existed before, but at the time of the queen's coronation there was at least a show of unity. Now, as the reality of having to cede a part of France began to sink in, people began to decide they didn't like the idea. One common and rather unpleasant trend in politics from the 1440s onwards was scapegoating, blaming all the perceived problems of the country on one person. In the first instance, it was William de la Pole, Duke of Suffolk, who alone was blamed for having made plans to hand Maine to the King of France. Few took account of the fact that ceding Maine had been part of a strategic initiative to protect English territory in France, relinquishing one area that was getting harder to defend in order to concentrate on retaining others, especially Normandy. The pursuit of peace had been something Henry himself supported from the outset, and he never objected to the plan.

There was also considerable resistance to the implementation of the plan within France itself, so that giving up Maine proved to be easier said than done. Henry VI formally sealed the agreement to surrender the county on 27 July 1447, but the plan did not run smoothly. By October English commanders were refusing to give up their positions without compensation. It is easy to see this as simple stubbornness by an 'occupying force', as historians like Nancy Goldstone have labelled them. However, many soldiers, especially those who formed the garrisons of major towns and cities, had long since settled in France. Many of them had married local women and raised families.[14] They were essentially part of the local population, and they were being asked to give up all they knew. They could not simply leave and return to a country they had not seen in decades.

An agreement had been made the previous year for the English to effectively pull out of Maine by 15 January 1448; the date came and went with little change. The county was still in English hands. The King of France therefore decided to take matters into his own hands, laying siege to its ancient capital city, Le Mans, in June. Finally, the English commanders had no choice but to leave, retreating for the most part to other English-held territories, although some returned to England.

The influx of veterans returning from France during the late 1440s and early 1450s was once speculated to have been a contributing factor to the later Wars of the Roses. This is unlikely, since a lot of these men would probably have been in their thirties or forties at this time, and the Wars of the Roses did not really begin until the late 1450s.

The sight of veterans returning – and not in triumph – certainly did nothing for the national mood. Chroniclers spoke of carts rolling through London stuffed with armour and household goods, with miserable women and children trailing behind in a 'piteous array' of humanity and a shameful display of what they saw as defeat and betrayal. Some of the men among these refugees seem to have ended up resorting to crime to survive when alms proved insufficient. They fell into what observers called 'theft and misrule', resulting in outbreaks of localized disorder and anti-refugee sentiment. These men were the soldiers who had formed the garrisons of major towns and cities in Maine, the troops who had been involved in engagements earlier on the war. They could not simply be sent back into the field as there was meant to be a truce with France. Here was another example of that eternal problem: soldiers with nothing to do.[15]

What made matters worse was that not all of the returning men came from the newly ceded Maine. Many in fact came from Normandy, the duchy that had belonged to the kings of England for centuries. By 1449, the King of France, buoyed by the return of Maine, declared war on the English and prepared for a full-scale invasion of Normandy which he enacted in July. By 29 October, Edmund Beaufort, Duke of Somerset and Lieutenant General of Normandy, had surrendered Rouen to the French after a short siege.

Rouen was effectively the capital of the region, and its surrender marked the loss of Normandy in spirit if not in fact. The duke was even shamefully forced to give up his own properties in Normandy as the price of his own freedom and hand over John Talbot, Earl of Shrewsbury as a hostage. He probably wasn't keen to keep the properties anyway, since by that time most of the duchy was back under French control. By 1 January 1450, Harfleur had fallen too. The news would not have been the most welcome New Year's gift for King Henry.

The situation in Maine had been compounded in 1447 by the death of Humphrey, Duke of Gloucester. The treatment of the king's paternal uncle in his last days was to prove one of the most controversial moments in Henry's reign. The duke had generally been opposed to the king's attempts to make peace with France since the outset and was outspoken against the surrender of Maine. As the younger brother of Henry V he was loyal to his nephew, but he could not sit by while Henry gave away what his brother had fought so hard to obtain. Notoriously, Humphrey was accused of 'treason' in the weeks before his death and was then found dead before charges could be brought against him. Arrested alongside Gloucester were several other individuals of his household. One of them was Arthur, the duke's own illegitimate son. Arthur of Gloucester is an elusive figure, his life and movements hard to trace. He was obviously still living in his father's household in his early twenties and seems to have died in July 1447, around the same time as his father.[16]

While it is entirely possible that Duke Humphrey died of natural causes (he was in his fifties and may have suffered a stroke, perhaps brought on by the shock of his arrest), the stones of the rumour mill soon began to turn. The convergence of disasters in the five years following Henry and Margaret's marriage had precipitated a collapse of both public and elite support. Courtiers had been supportive of a two-year truce with France, and perhaps not entirely hostile to the idea of ceding Maine with the hopes of gaining an advantage in the long term. However, what transpired was a virtual reconquest of the county, followed in short order by the loss of Normandy. Little attempt was made to even to fight back against the French, and insult was added to injury when veterans straggled home with their families after years spent serving in garrisons and in victorious armies. The sense of disaffection and betrayal was tangible. There were murmurings of discontent, whispers that perhaps Maine and Normandy had simply been *allowed* to fall without a fight. Had there been a conspiracy? People started to cast around looking for someone to blame.

They fell upon the Duke of Suffolk. Had he not been heavily involved in the king's marriage? Had he not been the architect of the plan to cede Maine? Had he not enthusiastically endorsed the idea, against the advice of men like Good Duke Humphrey? Obviously, the duke must have betrayed his country, its people and its soldiers, sold out to the enemy. He *must* have been a traitor. The scapegoating of Suffolk might seem natural at first, as he had indeed been heavily involved in the negotiations, but it is highly unlikely that he committed any kind of treason.

Quite the contrary. Suffolk had been acting at the behest of his king all the time, and had even at one point given a speech in Parliament insisting that the remaining English possessions in France should not be abandoned just because there was a truce, and that they should focus their attention on resupplying and maintaining existing fortresses and cities. Suffolk eloquently argued the case for his innocence in Parliament, but it was sadly too late. The recriminations were too far reaching and the people wanted blood.

On 7 February 1450, Suffolk was arrested and impeached for treason. Impeachment was a relatively uncommon procedure in the fifteenth century, which indicates the unusual nature of the charges. Usually when a person was accused of treason it was for an offence, intended or actual, against the person of the king, or for siding with his enemies. Impeachment was initiated and enacted by the Commons rather than the Lords, and was intended to deal with actions against the state or the nation. The treason in this case was supposed to involve corruption and colluding with a foreign power: the French. While the usual intent of impeachment was simply to remove a person from office, in

Suffolk's case it was to bring down upon him the full force of the law.

In Suffolk's case, the proceedings were long and drawn out. A whole series of charges were levelled against him. At the start it was the aforementioned accusations of colluding with the French for his own financial gain, but it proved hard to make these charges stick, and when the king tasked his own judges with investigating the matter it became even more difficult. Eventually, the allegations became more serious. Suffolk was accused of involvement in the supposed murder of Humphrey, Duke of Gloucester, of conniving so that the king was denied a wealthier and more prestigious bride, and even of embezzling funds. Some of the charges were sufficiently far-fetched to give the impression that they were being wholly fabricated, and that the Commons was simply determined to find something, anything, on which to hang a conviction. Finally, they made the most serious allegation of all: he had plotted to enthrone his son, whom he had recently betrothed to the only child and heiress of John Beaufort, Duke of Somerset.

It was basically at the discretion of the king to carry out the sentence in cases of impeachment, but the accusations the Commons were making against Suffolk went beyond the scope of impeachment. He was being accused of treason, and this required Henry to act. On 17 March, he called Suffolk to answer charges in person – not to be put on trial before the Lords, as was usual in cases of treason. This personal intervention (in which the young queen may have been involved) resulted in the king deeming his minister innocent of treason but guilty of the lesser offence of misprision. Henry therefore banished Suffolk from the realm for five years, passing sentence himself 'by his own advice and not resorting the to the advice of the Lords'.[17]

The king may have acted just in time, because at his trial Suffolk suggested that many other Lords had been involved in the cessation of Maine and that he alone could not possibly have done everything he was accused of. He was basically right, but it would have been extremely embarrassing for the others implicated if he'd gone all the way and named them in order to save himself. However, the lenient sentence did not appease the stirred-up peasantry, who wanted their scapegoat. The members of the House of Commons finished proceedings for impeachment outside Parliament. That gave them satisfaction at least. However, the ordinary people were not placated, and because of the presence of a mob in Westminster Suffolk had to be smuggled out of the palace, and the king had to prorogue Parliament in the hopes that they would disperse.

As May dawned, shortly after Suffolk's ship embarked for Calais, the people decided to take direct action against the hated royal minister. His ship was intercepted by a smaller vessel called *Nicholas of the Tower*. The captain ominously summoned Suffolk aboard, greeting him with the words, 'Welcome, traitor.' His letter of safe conduct from the king was torn up. The ship's crew then convened a mock trial for treason, after which the duke was beheaded with a rusty sword. It reportedly took half a dozen blows to sever his head. His body was unceremoniously dumped on a beach beneath the cliffs of Dover on 2 May. The chroniclers recounted this event in their typically partisan manner, saying that the 'evil' duke was 'arrested and brought to justice' as if the crew of the *Nicholas of the Tower* were exercising due process of law, not vigilante murder.

So where did Margaret factor into all of this? Sadly, she was tainted by association with the Duke of Suffolk. It was only natural that she would have had a close relationship with the man, since he was basically the first member of the English court she had known in France. Their friendship endured after Margaret came to England and married the king, probably lasting until the duke's murder. She was also a close personal friend of Suffolk's wife, Alice.

When the spin doctors began to say that Suffolk was a traitor and that he had sold out the country, the most tangible reminder of his hated Treaty of Troyes was the king's wife. People began to reframe what had happened in the last five years and say that Maine and Normandy had basically been sold for the queen, and they were regretting the exchange. Her association with Suffolk was known and, as was inevitable, rumours began to circulate that the young queen's friendship with Suffolk crossed the line of propriety and decency. The story began to circulate that Margaret had been romantically involved with the slain duke.

Another rumour was that Margaret herself was in fact illegitimate, the product of an affair during René's absence. This accusation reduced the young queen to tears in private, but there is no reason to believe it was true. The Suffolk insinuation would not be the last time that the queen's sexual morality was brought into question. Speculating about a woman's sex life was one of the most popular ways of undermining her reputation in the fifteenth century, especially if she was noble. It also reflects something of the insecurities of society during this period that the very worst accusation you could level at a landholder or someone in power was illegitimacy.

Sexual slurs aside, the most common accusation was that Margaret had in some way influenced policy towards France. Was she not in regular correspondence with her father, and even with her uncle the King of France? It is known that she did communicate with her relatives in France during the period of the truce between 1445 and 1447, so people began to assume that she was intentionally working against English interests as an enemy within. This is why, from 1450 onwards, we start to see more openly critical and even hostile statements about the young queen. Everything that went wrong in France –indeed, anything occurring in England that could be tied to it – must have had something to do with the queen and a circle of nobles around her.

Poor Margaret was in an untenable situation. She was still only in her teens before 1450, and anything she did to help maintain the Treaty of Tours she would have seen as her duty, both to her family and to her husband and his people. She considered herself to be duty bound to try and sustain good relations between her homeland and her husband's country. This harked back to the ancient role of a queen as a mediator and weaver of peace. It didn't directly benefit her to intentionally undermine the interests of either country, despite what is often claimed.

However, she might well have inadvertently encouraged the agreement between the two kings. Henry VI certainly seems to have made a quiet verbal agreement with Charles over the cession of Maine; it was not, as is assumed, a formal part of the marriage contract. Although the king only actually visited France once, when he was eight years old, he could convey his wishes through intermediaries such as the Duke of Suffolk. It was not so much the case that the king was willing to give up land because he so desperately wanted Margaret that he would do anything for her; rather he wanted peace, and was willing to make himself unpopular to achieve it. Margaret's continued correspondence with her 'very dear uncle' was part of this. She had written to him in May 1446 that she would 'help to the best of our power to direct and rectify the matters which shall be treated between you two' in a meeting that was to be held between the two monarchs (or their representatives). She also claimed that the meeting would bring about 'a fruitful conclusion in the matter of general peace which we desire ... above all earthly things'.[18]

Margaret's correspondence between 1445 and 1447 may have seemed innocuous to her. She was simply trying to do her part to bring about a truce with France and mediating between her uncle and husband. Laynesmith argues that Margaret did not have any actual role in these negotiations beyond writing a few letters, and they did not change much since the King of England had already made up his mind on the matter. Her uncle was trying to tie her more closely to her new country or else he was just stringing her along.[19] If anyone was being played, it was Henry and Margaret. The King of France wanted to press the King of England to give up Maine, to keep his promise without delaying, and decided to work on his niece to try to pressurise him into doing so. The teenage queen was simply torn between the two and wanted to please everyone.

She could not.

The only way that the cession of Maine could have been forgiven or made to look worthwhile would have been if the English had won the war and held onto the rest of their lands in France for many generations. Unfortunately for Margaret, that was not the case, and so her every action during the 1440s came to be interpreted in an unfavourable light. Instead of just trying to broker a peace deal, the queen was said to have been treacherously undermining the interests of England. Instead of her marriage being part of a wider effort to bring about an end to the war, it was said that the English had sold out to France.

Either way, the events of 1450, beginning with Suffolk's murder, are considered by modern historians to have been the crisis that sparked off the conflict that would become known as the Wars of the Roses. According to Professor Michael Hicks, public engagement in politics like that seen in the Suffolk debacle would come to characterise the second half the fifteenth century. The people had been determined to get rid of Suffolk, and his mild treatment by the king even prompted an abortive rising in London led by a servant called John Frammesley, who spread a rhyme suggesting that the king would lose his crown because of what had happened. In hindsight his words proved to be prophetic.

The crisis of January to March 1450 led directly to another period of violent upheaval later on in the year. Tensions were high after Suffolk's murder, with the commons of Kent expecting reprisals from the enraged monarch. No matter how justified they might have felt in what they had done to Suffolk, there was very little precedent for the execution of a royal minister and peer of the realm by the commons. Such a thing had only happened before during wider insurrections and uprisings.

Jack Cade's rebellion, as the event has come to be known, grew out of this. Just over a month after Suffolk's murder on 6 June 1450 'some men rose in rebellion in Kent'. They chose as their leader 'a most bold and subtle man Jack Cade, who called himself John Mortimer'. Cade led a contingent of 4,000 from Kent and Sussex to London. The rebellion has many parallels with the Peasants' Revolt that had occurred over sixty years before; it was even preceded by the approval of a tax by Parliament.

Cade's rebellion was no less violent. When the thousands of rebels descended upon Blackheath in late May, the king was still in Leicester. On 6 June he sent several nobles south arrayed for war. They advised the king not to come until they had ascertained the size of the rebel host and its demands. The king himself followed soon afterwards, presumably upon receiving word that it was safe to do so. On 16 June he sent John Stafford, Archbishop of Canterbury and Chancellor of England, and Cardinal Kempe to parley with the rebels and hear their terms.

Their grievances all related to abuses in government and the competency of some of the king's key advisors. They were also angry about high taxes and the recent loss of Normandy. These complaints were set out in what came to be known as a 'petition', which was the best term as it made them sound like loyal subjects beseeching the king rather than traitors.

Item, they say that whom ye kyng will shall be traitor and whom he will shall be non, and that appearth hitherto for if any of the traitors about him would malign against any person, high or low, they would find false means that he should die a traitor for to have his lands and his goods, but they will suffer the king neither to pay his debts withall, nor pay for his victuals ner be the richer of one penny.

Item, the law serveth of naught else in these days but for to do wrong, for nothyng is sped almost but false maters by colour of the law for mede, drede, and favor, and so no remedy is had in ye court of conscience in any wise.

Item, we say our sovereign lord may understand that his false council hath lost his law, his merchandise is lost, his common people is destroyed, the see is lost, France is lost, the king himself is so set that he may not pay for his mete nor drinke, and he oweth more than ever any King of England ought, for daily his traitors about him where anything should come to hym by his laws, anon they aske it from hym.

Item, his trewe comyns desireth that he will avoid from him all the false progeny and affinity of the Duke of Suffolk, the which ben openly known, and that they be punished after law of land.[20]

These three items reveal the rebels' key grievances: the decline of law and order, misrule, corruption and financial instability, along with the customary lamenting at the loss of French territory.

The king's negotiators offered the rebels a pardon if they would go home, but they stood resolute, insisting that the king answer their demands in person. He refused both their demands and their summons. Then, in an act of ruthless resolve seldom associated with the mild Henry, he sent in the soldiers. The following day, 17 June, the king himself marched from Clerkenwell with a large group of retainers 'in full military array with banners raised'.[21] It is ironic that this would be the first and the only time that he would (willingly) march out at the head of an army, and it was against his own people.

The show of military force was intended to cow the rebels. If they resisted their king with his banners raised, they would automatically be guilty of treason. Yet by the time they reached Blackheath, there was nobody there. The rebels had already dispersed. Most had fled during the night, presumably having been tipped off. Henry soon departed for Greenwich Palace, where Margaret waited, but he left his forces on standby at Blackheath to guard against the rebels' return.

Not all of the troops were ordered to stay put. Henry dispatched a small force, including two Stafford kinsmen of the Duke of Buckingham, to hunt down the rebels. This is another instance of uncharacteristic decisiveness from the king, but one that, in a foreshadowing of the later conflicts of his reign, was to prove disastrous. The Stafford party was ambushed by rebels and wiped out in a narrow lane near Sevenoaks, Kent. News of the victory spread quickly, and when it reached the ears of the royal forces stationed at Blackheath many deserted or rose up in outright munity. There might have been more to this mutiny than the mere victory over one division of the king's troops, however; he had sent out several divisions, and one of them was reportedly ravaging the Kent countryside. The notion of soldiers treating their countrymen in this way might have been enough to turn some.

Not only had Henry failed to quell the rebellion, but he was now faced with another among his own forces. Newly bolstered by victory, Cade's men were set to gather again, joined by the very troops who had been meant to keep them at bay.

Henry had no choice but to go along with their demands; his people would turn against him if he did not 'do execution to his traitors'. He was forced to send to the Tower several of the nobles named in Cade's petition, among them James Fiennes, Lord Saye, but he did not proceed against them for treason. With rebels still abroad in London and disaffection reportedly spreading even as far as the royal court, King Henry decided to abandon the capital.

He took many of his court with him, but he left the queen behind.

This need not be read as a callous act. Henry was staying with Margaret in Greenwich in late June while the rebels were regrouping, and it is thought that she might have been working to have Lord Saye pardoned or quietly released during that time. The queen had not been threatened by the rebels, and she could stay in communication with the members of the royal retinue who were still in London. This suggests that Margaret may have been playing some role in government at least behind the scenes somewhat earlier than is usually thought.

The king withdrew to Kenilworth, and the rebels once again gathered at Blackheath on 2 July. From there they marched into London and chaos ensued. Previously, Cade had been happy to wait for an answer from the king. He'd expressly stated he did not want to hurt anyone, but in the early days of July he lost control of the thousands under his nominal leadership. The rebels went on the rampage, pillaging, killing and wreaking havoc in the capital. On 4 July they extricated John Crowmer, Sheriff of Kent, from the Fleet and beheaded him. At the same time, Lord Saye was being indicted by royal justices, and he too was eventually handed over to the rebels and beheaded. His body was despoiled and dragged through London in a gruesome display.

The commons had exacted 'justice' once again, but this time the people of London turned against them. Cade had promised no violence. On 5 July, they decided to take a stand and prevent the rebels from re-entering London. Fighting broke out on London Bridge. The Londoners prevailed and the rebels were driven back. The court then made a timely intervention, offering a pardon to Jack Cade on the 6th and to all the other rebels on the 7th. They seem to have dispersed quickly thereafter.

The pardon may have come from Cardinal Kemp, who was himself a Kentishman. It is unlikely to have come from the king, who was still holed up at Kenilworth. It is possible that Queen Margaret may also have had something to do with it. She may even have worked on the king himself when he was in London, because his attitude towards the rebels was not conciliatory at first. He had been prepared to come against them in arms, but later changed his tune. Regardless of her personal feelings, it was vital that pardons be issued to encourage the rebels to disperse. Nobody wanted all-out war on the streets of the capital, and rebel leaders could always be punished at a later date. It was also consistent with the ancient duties of a queen to act as intercessor and giver of mercy between the people and her husband.

Unsurprisingly, Jack Cade was hunted down despite his pardon. A man like him would never have been allowed to go free. The newly appointed Sheriff of Essex 'and many others' went in pursuit of him and a few days after the dispersal of the rebellion, on 12 July, 'came upon him beside the sea and killed him'.[22] They brought his body back to London and had the corpse beheaded and quartered, the traditional treatment for a commoner convicted of treason. His limbs were distributed among Kentish towns.

If King Henry and the rest of the court believed they could now breathe easily, they were to be disappointed. The year was marked with further local uprisings or attempted insurrections, most of them involving people railing against the king's 'evil ministers'. The people of Kent and Essex tried to rise again shortly afterwards, but this rebellion was soon quelled by the arrival of the Duke of Buckingham, Cardinal Kempe and the Archbishop of Canterbury as well as a newly commissioned royal justice to 'hold eyre', a local court. This court was intended to investigate the people's local grievances and settle disputes so that they would be less likely to rebel. The choice of the three men was significant because the two bishops had been responsible for drawing up the pardons for those involved in Cade's rebellion, and Buckingham had been one of the envoys who had met with Cade earlier in the year.

An intriguing letter survives from late 1450 which shows another of Margaret's personal interventions on behalf of someone who had approached her. The tenacious and partisan nature of this correspondence is notable. Margaret began writing to the mayor and aldermen of London in October 1450 to ask them to reinstate one Alexander Manning as the keeper of Newgate gaol. Manning had been expelled from this position amid allegations of negligence; it seems that when the Duke of York had entered the city in September Manning had marked the occasion by releasing several prisoners, who then refused to return to confinement. A riot ensued in which a visitor was attacked. Manning was expelled by the mayor, who had to muster men to round up the recalcitrant inmates. Manning appealed to a relative, Thomas Manning, who was the king's chaplain, and word reached the queen, who decided to try to get her man reinstated.

Understandably, her request was denied, and Manning was firmly told that he would not be reinstated. Yet just under a year later, Margaret wrote again to the mayor and to the elected sheriffs under him extolling Manning's virtues and asserting that she was still interested in his case. Her attempt was once again unsuccessful. Why was the queen so interested in having somebody who was apparently so incompetent reinstated to a position of trust? It is possible that Margaret considered personal connections to be more important than a person's mistakes, or that she was willing to overlook a person's faults and shortcomings (even serious ones) if they were loyal to her and prepared to do her bidding. Manning was related to a royal chaplain, someone who was obviously in a position of trust, so she may have trusted the man as well. By having him in charge of Newgate perhaps she felt that he could protect her interests and those of the crown better. What was a little prison riot, provided he was not allowing rebels to go on the rampage, or worse still letting them out, if another group of rebellious commons came out in force baying for the blood of her friends? Margaret was also showing her determined streak when she 'ran head on against the determined independence of the London city government'.[23]

In November, despite Parliament being convened for the second time that year, 'a thousand men' rose with the intent of killing the Duke of Somerset, whom they had by now come to blame for the loss of France.[24] He was being blamed for the surrender of Harfleur and he had personally surrendered the Norman city of Caen to the French in July, followed by Cherbourg in August. Even if there was no more hope of holding the territory, the general who surrendered it was always personally blamed. Fabyan's chronicle reported rumours circulating that Somerset and some his fellow generals in Normandy had accepted money to surrender cities in the region.[25] This is unlikely to have actually been the case, but it shows the refusal among the ordinary people to accept that the French were simply able to defeat the English forces. An English lack of will to fund the war, combined with the strength and stability of the French regime and their changing tactics all contributed to France gaining the upper hand, but none of this was taken into account. As far as the people were concerned, the loss of so much territory *must* have been an act of betrayal.

At the second 1450 parliament 'an apprentice at law' by the name of Thomas Younge declared that because the king had no heirs the Duke of York should be declared his legal successor. This was a step too far. It was down to the king himself to designate his heir; it was not determined by popular vote. Younge was committed to the Tower in short order. Nonetheless, it may already be observed that people were beginning to favour the idea of the Duke of York either becoming the heir to the childless monarch or becoming king himself. In the four years since the death of his uncle and nearest blood relative, the duke had come to seem the logical choice when measured against the unpopular Somerset.

At the same time, the common folk showed a vindictive streak by demanding that various royal servants be removed from their posts and punished. Curiously, one of them was Alice Chaucer, the widow of the Duke of Suffolk. There were calls for Suffolk to be posthumously attainted, which would have deprived Alice of her dower and disinherited her son. Further still, they insisted that she be tried for treason. This was almost unprecedented. Women were not tried for high treason. We might associate the Tudors with such behaviour (it is often said that the Plantagenets did not execute women), but it appears that we can see the beginning of the change here.[26]

This new mob was pacified by the Earl of Devon, who arrested their leader, and some of the common people among the group degenerated to looting and ransacking a local friary. To quell the violence and set an example, the Duke of York had one of them handed over to the king, who in turn had him beheaded. Presumably, this group dispersed shortly afterwards, as no more is heard of their activities. This does give us an interesting insight into Henry, suggesting that he was in fact capable of acting decisively when pushed.

On 3 December, the king, with all the nobles, knights and squires, 'accompanied by some well-armed soldiers to the number of about ten thousand marched through London'.[27] This was a show of power and royal authority that was presumably intended to cow anyone in the city with rebellious intentions. This had proved to be an especially turbulent year both for Henry and for the wider political establishment, with some troubling implications. The king, as historian Lauren Johnson writes, had always held great faith in the goodwill of his fellow men, especially his countrymen. Never had he faced outright rebellion, let alone the murder of several of his closest advisors.

It wasn't just among the commoners that trouble was brewing in 1450 either. Feuds among the nobility were going unchecked, notably the Percy–Neville vendetta in the north. In the summer England was forced to surrender Le Mans, and in August Richard, Duke of York returned from his duties in Ireland without leave. Despite later chroniclers and dramatists' inventions, there had been no indication of any animosity between the king and the duke before 1450. However, Jack Cade as mentioned had taken on the name Mortimer (York's mother was a Mortimer) and we are already aware of the whisperings about replacing Henry with York, who after the death of the Duke of Gloucester had come to be regarded by some as his best successor. A clerk's note blamed York for the situation in the country: 'From the time that Jack Cade or Mortimer, called captain of Kent, raised a rebellion in Kent, all disturbances are at the will of the Duke of York, descended from the Mortimers.' Clearly, the common people were not the only ones playing the blame game.

Between September and October, the king and York exchanged a series of letters, with the latter professing his loyalty to the king while stressing that he was not involved in the events of the summer.

> Since my departure out of your realm by your command, and being in your service in your land of Ireland, I have been informed that language has been used about me in your presence [to] my dishonour and reproach ... In spite of this, I have been, and ever shall be, your true liegeman and servant.

Considering he had been in Ireland for the duration of the trouble, this is credible enough. However, we can see in these missives the beginning of York's problems with other nobles, especially his erstwhile rival Edmund Beaufort, Duke of Somerset. He also begins to echo the protests of the commons.

> May it please your highness to consider indulgently the great complaining and rumour that is universal throughout this realm, to the effect that justice is not duly administered to such as trespass and offend against your laws, especially [regarding] those who are indicted of treason and others who have been openly accused of the same. On account of this great troubles have befallen, and are likely to befall hereafter, your realm, unless suitable provision is made by your highness for due reformation and punishment in this matter.

Subsequently, York graciously offered to help the king execute justice upon these people and bring justice to his realm. The king declined, but the duke did get what he wanted in one sense: in December 1450, Somerset was committed to the Tower of London after an attempt was made on his life. This was ostensibly done for his own safety, but more likely it was designed to appease the mob that had interrupted Parliament.

In early 1451 the King was reported to have gone to Canterbury alongside several of his nobles and justices, where they 'held judicial sessions four days'. Basically, these were court proceedings presided over by the royal justices and held to decide the fate of various men who had been involved in Cade's rebellion, as well as others who had been 'speaking against the King, having more favour towards the Duke of York than the King'.[28] These men were condemned to the brutal punishment of being hanged, drawn and quartered, the penalty for a treasonous commoner. Here again we see a different Henry VI to the image often proffered; his justice came to be known as the 'harvest of heads'.[29]

Henry's credibility as a monarch had taken a major blow in 1450, and the unrest was still simmering below the surface.[30] Alongside concerns about the government, the war in France was continuing to go badly, and the royal coffers were also a serious cause for concern. Henry VI maintained a very large household of around 800 individuals. This was larger than that of most of his predecessors and put enormous strain on finances. Servants had to be fed and paid, and nobles were entitled to partake of their lord's hospitality despite being able to afford to pay for their food and upkeep.[31]

The king's generosity in the granting of offices 'and all the possessions and lordships relating to the crown' had placed him badly in debt. Most kings were in debt, however;[32] it was rare indeed for them not to be. Indeed, subjects expected lords to be generous with patronage instead of 'holding onto their purse', in other words being miserly. Miserliness was even considered to be a sin by the church. On the other hand, King Henry's patronage was said to be biased, with offices heaped upon his favourites and relatives while others were ignored. It isn't hard though to assume that in a way the king was stuck between a rock and a hard place and could not possibly please all of his subjects. Not without the morale boost of victory in war or something similar, at least.

The financial problems that beset the wider kingdom at this time did not even have their origins in the country. There was a recession sweeping over most of Europe during this period, and England was not immune. Michael Hicks described this period as an economic depression which had first appeared when the Black Death began to bite. In England it has been dubbed the Great Slump and it lasted for forty years, beginning in 1440. Hicks identified the major cause as a decrease in the production of goods after the plague and a critical shortage of silver bullion, 'which meant that actual coins and the credit necessary for trade were lacking'.[33] This led to protectionist measures that in turn affected trade, which was extremely important to the English economy even then. Hicks goes on to relate how the Great Slump affected all areas of society from 'the high nobility, whose rents fell, especially in the Welsh marches, and whose costs rose. It hit cultivators, whose products sold for less if at all, manufacturers who encountered falling demand, artisans who were underemployed or unemployed, and landholders who could not lease their lands or collect their rents.'

The two worst affected groups were sheep farmers and cloth workers. Sheep farming was mostly concentrated in the Cotswolds and Wiltshire. Significantly, the major exporters of cloth were based in Kent, home to the rebels of 1450. The county was a trading hub and was severely impacted by the Great Slump. This spilled over into London, where foreign trade was lifeblood, as the city was filled with craftsmen and tradespeople and traders in luxury goods. In fact, it has been argued that there was a major overlap between the regions most involved in the violence of 1450–52 and areas central to foreign trade and the wool trade: Sussex, Kent and London. Londoners typically blamed problems on 'foreigners'; such xenophobic sentiments had been the norm for centuries. When there was unrest or discontent in the capital, foreigners suffered. It is not that much of a leap of the imagination to consider that the French-born queen may have been caught up in some of this hate and mistrust.

Indeed, some of the more unflattering whisperings about Margaret have their origins in this time period, although most are later. Margaret was only really an acceptable target at that time as the 'foreign queen' and the potential enemy within, but that would soon change.

Economic woes were further exacerbated by the challenge of prosecuting a war that people were not willing to fund or fight but which they still expected to win. There was the taxation necessary to sustain the conflict. Even the slightest tax was regarded as an unacceptable hardship by the commons of Kent and Sussex, who were already struggling with unsold goods and plunging prices. The idea that the king was frittering away money or that the government ministers were corrupt was the final straw for them.

The Duke of Somerset was released from the Tower in April 1451, coinciding with another attempted armed rising in Kent. He was also made Captain of Calais and the queen herself gave him a salary of 100 marks 'for good service and friendship'. They were probably also compensation for his six months or so spent in the Tower. Even this was used against poor Margaret as she was now seen to be associating herself with the increasingly unpopular duke. Once again, gossip and rumours of an inappropriate relationship between the pair began to circulate. Edmund Beaufort himself had once been associated with Katherine de Valois, King Henry VI's mother. He was said to have been the reason why Parliament forbade her from marrying without royal consent; after all, as the first cousin of Henry V, any child he might have had with Queen Katherine could have been a threat to Henry VI.

Some twenty-five years later, whispers associated the man of nearly fifty, whose eldest son was in his teens, with Margaret. They were, like most such rumours, almost certainly false. There is no logical reason to assume that any relationship Margaret (or any other woman) had with a man was sexual, and besides, she was with the king most of the time. If anything, it is more likely that Margaret, who was still only twenty-one, regarded Somerset as a father figure. With that said, one may question the wisdom of the queen rewarding the man who had surrendered a French city the year before. The people certainly did. It was probably a simple courtesy, designed to help a friend, but in the prevailing atmosphere of paranoia it didn't go down well.

With Normandy fallen, in the spring of 1451 Charles of France started to set his sights on the last remaining English possession that side of the Channel: Gascony. The duchy in the south-west of the country roughly compromised parts of what had once been known as Aquitaine. Bordeaux and Bayonne were surrendered in June and August respectively, but the region was not completely taken by the end of the year.

By some miracle, or perhaps because Henry had been able to assert his authority in the kingdom, he and Margaret were able to enjoy a happy Christmas in 1451 at their favourite palace of Greenwich. It has not survived, but it was probably located on the modern site of Greenwich University and the Royal Observatory. Humphrey, Duke of Gloucester had obtained a licence to redevelop his manor on the site; there had been a royal manor house there since the thirteenth century (perhaps earlier), and the duke's work seems to have been extensive, including the addition of a tower and crenelation. It came to include kitchens, chapels, an armoury and even a tiltyard for jousting events. To assure luxury, it was set in nearly 200 acres of parklands and had orchards and gardens. After the duke was accused of treason in 1447 the palace was taken back into royal hands, much in the way that Henry VIII would later take possession of Hampton Court Palace from Cardinal Wolsey. Margaret renamed the palace Placentia, or Pleasaunce, and it seems to have been her favourite retreat whenever she was in London.

As 1452 dawned, Henry's determination to reassert his authority and to address the grievances of his people had not faded. Unfortunately for him, his problems hadn't either. Two major cities in Gascony had been lost. The Duke of Somerset was out of the Tower and the Duke of York, his sense of entitlement as great as ever, felt under threat. In February, together with Thomas Courtenay, Earl of Devon and Lord Cobham, York emerged from his estate in the Welsh marches with an army. Some chronicles report that they might have raised as many as 20,000 men between them. The Courtenay earls of Devon are known to have been staunch Lancastrians, and so one of them siding with York in 1452 seem strange, but he had worked with the duke before. He had also been engaged for nearly a decade in a bitter and violent feud with William, 1st Baron Bonville, another West Country nobleman. Courtenay may have sided with York in this instance because he had been protecting him from Bonville. Whatever the reason, the three nobles and their forces rode to Northampton, where the king sent the Bishop of Winchester to treat with them.

York was firmly told that he must not raise arms against the crown. No matter what his excuses or his justifications, raising arms against the king in any capacity was treason as far as the law was concerned. No ifs, no buts. York sought to justify his actions in the manner now typical: he was a loyal subject who would not dream of raising arms against his sovereign and was simply acting for the good of the country to get rid of the people responsible for bad governance who had betrayed the king. *He* wasn't the traitor; he was coming to get the traitors. He had sworn an oath saying as much on the Holy Sacrament on 9 January.

The king didn't buy it for a second. As York's forces marched south, Henry ordered the mayor of London to forbid him entry. This he did, so York's army was forced to take a roundabout route via Kingston, staying there for three days before moving on to Dartford, where on 29 February he 'took up a position strongly fortified ... with posts, ditches and guns and awaited the opportunity to enter the king's presence'.[34] York had merely come to talk to the king – with a big army for his own protection, naturally.

The king responded in kind, arriving at the head of an army and encamping at Blackheath. Later sources claimed that when York arrived to see the king, he met with a surprise: his enemy the Duke of Somerset, whose arrest he had demanded when he had parleyed with the Bishop of Winchester days before. York was at an impasse. He still wanted the king to meet his demands, but he did not dare rise against him in anger. That would be outright treason. Furthermore, York was finding that his support was waning. His forces were melting away, and the people of London were not rallying to his cause as he had hoped. He was faced with the king and many of his lords, who boasted superior numbers and more support, and they were threatening to bring the full force of the law down upon him. York had no choice but to capitulate.

On 2 March, York and the king were reconciled at Blackheath. It is recorded that York and his allies knelt before the king. He still took the opportunity to complain about the Duke of Somerset and the loss of France, but he was in no position to make demands. From Blackheath the king and the duke returned to the city of London, where York was made to swear a solemn oath before the king and the high altar of St Paul's Cathedral. He declared that he had 'never rebelled against the king and would never take up arms against him again'.[35] The oath was a little more detailed than this; it also involved promises not to gather armed men without the king's permission, nor to take any kind of direct action against his adversaries, and to resist those who would.

Not satisfied by private assurances, the king had insisted upon this public declaration of loyalty. But the oath in St Paul's was significant for more than just its public nature. It was sworn while touching the Bible, or the cross on the high altar of the church, and just before receiving the sacrament. To medieval sensibilities, this was the most solemn and binding type of oath. To perjure oneself was more than just dishonourable, it was a sin. It was like lying to God himself.

After the Dartford incident, the king continued to entrench his authority. That summer he went on a progress through the West Country with Somerset and a few others while Margaret stayed at Greenwich in the longest period of separation they had experienced in seven years of marriage. Later rumours about her having an affair with the much older Somerset cannot be substantiated, and the fact that he was on progress with the king in the summer of 1452 certainly rules out the possibility at this time.

While on progress, the king was again making a show of his power. There were several instances of men being sentenced to death and then pardoned in a show of royal mercy. He even made a visit to Lord Bonville, taking a side in the feud with Courtenay. Henry was trying to address the grievances of his subjects and provide good rule by hearing cases and punishing traitors and rebels. Why did he not do more about Somerset? Likely because the duke had committed no treason, and York had no right to demand he be punished purely based on personal animosity.

Henry was also making a concerted effort to defend England's interests in France. On 17 October, the seasoned English commander John Talbot was dispatched on an expedition to retake Gascony, much of which had fallen to the French in the previous year. Talbot was in his sixties, having been born in the same year as Henry V, but was still one of the best commanders in England. He managed to quickly retake Bordeaux, allowing the king to end 1452 on a positive note. Enjoying Christmas at her favourite palace with her family, Margaret surely hoped the future was bright. Certainly the year would begin with great promise. Sometime during the spring, Margaret realised that all her prayers had been answered. After nearly eight years of marriage, she was pregnant.

3

THE FRENCH QUEEN

By April 1453, it was clear to Margaret that she was finally *enceinte*. We know this because it is recorded that Richard Tunstall, the queen's chamberlain, received from the king a very generous annuity of forty marks as a gift for having told him of the queen's pregnancy.[1] After this, one of Margaret's first acts was to go to the shrine of the Virgin Mary at Walsingham to give thanks. The shrine was said to have been a scale replica of the house in Nazareth in the Holy Land where the Angel Gabriel announced to the Virgin that she would give birth to the saviour of the world, the Annunciation. She gave a gift there as thanks to the Mother of Christ for her intercession and help in conceiving; medieval Christianity was an interesting and eclectic affair in which cults sprang up around favoured saints, and Margaret seems to have had a particular devotion to the Virgin.

On the way back from Walsingham in April 1453, Margaret went to see her friend Cecily Neville, Duchess of York. Cecily responded to news of Margaret's pregnancy with enthusiastic and heartfelt congratulations, describing it as 'the most precious most joyful and most comfortable earthly treasure that might come unto this land and to the people thereof'.[2]

Some might be surprised to hear about the cordial relationship between the two women given the tensions between their husbands, but there is no evidence for any animus at this time. Indeed, there is a tendency to suggest a hostility between individuals of the houses of York and Lancaster which is simply not apparent in the 1440s or even the 1450s. Apart from the Duke of Somerset and some feuding families there does not seem to have been any acrimony between the royals and nobles of England. Cecily herself was the daughter of Joan Beaufort, one of the daughters of John of Gaunt and Katherine Swynford, and as such was the first cousin of King Henry V and a Lancastrian by blood. She was only a member of the House of York by marriage. She did, however, use Margaret's stay at her house at Hitchin in Hampshire as an opportunity to ask the queen to have a word with the king on her husband's behalf. York himself was keeping his head down and his tail between his legs following the Dartford incident the previous year.

Margaret's pregnancy has become the subject of much debate and speculation both in our time and her own. Certain historians have promoted the idea that Henry VI could not possibly have been the father of Margaret's child and that it *must* have been illegitimate. This idea has gained a lot of traction in recent years through writers such as John Ashdown-Hill and Philippa Gregory. One story that is often recounted as 'evidence' for the dubious paternity of Margaret's child is the claim that as soon as King Henry saw the boy, named Edward, he said that he was conceived of the Holy Spirit.

This story comes down to us via a second- or third-hand account by way of Prospero de Camulio, a Milanese ambassador who recounted the anecdote to his employer in 1461. So, it is late, and almost certainly Yorkist in origin. Even Camulio did not state its provenance; quite possibly it was just some gossip he had heard at the English court or even from English visitors to France (he was corresponding with a French nobleman).[3] In fact, he himself did not seem to believe it, so it can safely be concluded that the story is neither credible nor proven.

In the context of medieval sensibilities and what we know about Henry's piety, the rumour is almost certainly nonsense. To proclaim that anyone was conceived as the result of a virgin birth through the Holy Spirit was blasphemy. What this story was really doing was subverting the idea of the pious Henry into a man who was so religious as to be gullible and naïve. It has basically been successful, because such an image of Henry is widely accepted even today. He might have been pious and easily led, but he was not stupid.

Another story is that the date of Margaret's pregnancy does not add up. John Ashdown-Hill speculated that conception occurred in the summer of 1453, probably sometime around July or August. We know that Margaret gave birth to a son whom she would name Edward on 17 October 1453. If he was conceived in April or May, that would mean he was born at just five or six months. Babies born so prematurely did not generally survive in the fifteenth century. The notion that Prince Edward was conceived in August is even more absurd, as she would have been barely two months along in October. Unless Margaret contrived some sort of complicated plan to make her pregnancy seem further along than it was, and pretended to give birth in October, this story can safely be discounted as well. Medieval queens were seldom alone, surrounded as they were by servants, and such an elaborate deception would have required the complicity of many people.

There is no evidence that Henry himself was incapable of fathering a child, nor that he was so pious as to lack the desire to do so, as has been frequently claimed. Henry knew full well that it was his duty as a king to marry and produce an heir, despite allegations that one of his friends had discouraged him from sleeping with his wife. Specifically, it was said as early as 1447 that his confessor, William Aiscough, Bishop of Salisbury, had encouraged him not to share a bed with his wife. However, since Aiscough was later the target of popular anger as part of Suffolk's circle this may have been simple gossip. There was no logical reason for the bishop to have encouraged the king to stay away from his wife unless he wished for him to leave no heirs, which was probably the reason for the rumour. The idea that the advisor and confessor was somehow harming the king's legacy, and by extension threatening the future of the entire kingdom, played right into popular fears and prejudices.[4]

Even if Henry was as chaste as sometimes suggested, this did not rule out sex within marriage. There was a case of a couple who were described as chaste and yet had no fewer than nine children between them. The term could simply refer to a person who did not sleep around and was not inclined to cheat on their spouse. Such was the case with Henry VI. As such, there seems to be no basis on which to assume that Margaret had become pregnant by anyone other than her husband. Margaret was still only twenty-three years old in 1453, and today it would not be considered at all unreasonable or suspicious for a woman to have her first pregnancy at that age. Yet Margaret had been married for eight years, and previous queens had given birth to two or three children by her age. This was one thing Margaret and Cecily Neville had in common, for the latter did not give birth to her first child until she had been married for fourteen years.

Johnson speculates that one thing which may have delayed Margaret's pregnancy was her piety. Analysis of her household accounts suggests that she had taken to fasting several times a week. This was done for religious reasons, usually as part of a vow. Ironically, Margaret may well have been doing this in the hopes of becoming pregnant alongside praying and petitioning her favourite Saints and the Virgin. We know that Margaret suffered from ill-health before her wedding to Henry, which may have resulted from what we would now understand to have been severe anxiety and stress. Could these symptoms have also contributed to her failure to conceive earlier as well? She certainly suffered enough stress in the early 1450s.

In February 1453, just before realizing she was pregnant, Margaret received some tragic news. Word was sent from her father in France that her mother, Isabella of Lorraine, had died following a long illness. To realise that she was carrying a child less than two months after losing her beloved mother would have added a bittersweet tinge to the happy news.⁵ Isabella may have had less of an influence on Margaret's childhood than her grandmother Yolande, but she was still a strong and capable woman in keeping with the tradition of the Angevin family. Margaret took to wearing dark blue, which was then the colour associated with mourning, to mark her mother's passing. She may well have been in mourning when she realised she was pregnant; perhaps that is why she did not tell the king in person.

Another sting in the tail arrived in the summer with the end of the war in France. John Talbot, the veteran commander, had been sent on his expedition to retake Gascony the year before. It had begun with great hopes – even King Henry himself had spoken of perhaps wanting to lead an expedition to France like his father before him. It seems the French had been expecting the English to land in Normandy and were taken by surprise when they ended up landing in Guyenne. On the night of 22/23 October, Talbot took Bordeaux. While this victory may have been famous, there is some suggestion that the city was actually taken as a result of treachery, 'with the help of collaborators who opened the gate ... to the invaders'.[6]

By the spring of 1453 Talbot had been joined by his son, Viscount Lisle. He now had a force of about 7,000 men with which to take on the might of the French army. This was just as well, for the French were approaching. In summer they marched on Bordeaux from the north and west. In June, Talbot sent a challenge to one of the French commanders, but they were not ready to fight. Massively outnumbered, Talbot withdrew to Calais where he hoped to be reinforced from across the Channel. Two weeks passed with no relief. In turned out that when Parliament sat in the spring it had not even voted on whether or not to send any troops. On 8 July, one of the French commanders, Jean Bereau, laid siege to a nearby town called Castillon-sur-Dordogne. A sharp military mind, he laid out the French camp to make best use of his artillery with a defensive ditch.

The commander of the English garrison had begged for Talbot's help, and so he felt duty bound to relieve the siege. He set out with his forces on 16 July, arriving the next day. What became known as the Battle of Castillon ended with the English routed, and Talbot and his son dead.

The English loss at the battle of Castillon represented more than just a defeat. Talbot was really the last commander capable of mounting a serious campaign in France. It also 'destroyed the only English army capable of putting up resistance to the French in the field'.[7] Most of the other commanders headed home and seemed to have no particular desire to return to the field; others were just bickering among themselves. The battle practically marked the end of the conflict which is known as the Hundred Years War today. There were no more major battles, and England was never able to regain the lands which were lost in France. Only Calais remained in English hands. This was also the year in which Constantinople, once the capital of the Byzantine Empire, finally fell to the Ottoman Turks. Things were changing in Europe.

Castillon's effect on English morale was catastrophic, for the king as well as the general public. In early August, a few days after news of the defeat and Talbot's death reached him, King Henry suffered a total breakdown. In the middle of the night he 'was smitten with a frenzy and his wit and reason withdrawn'. At least that is what one source said. Others suggest he was taken ill in the opening days of August. The English Chronicle gives a more detailed description of what happened, saying that he 'took a sudden and unexpected fright'. While some suggest that the onset of the king's illness was so sudden that his servants found him unable to move one morning, others suggest it was more progressive and that his condition degenerated over a period of several days.

What we do know is that the symptoms were dramatic and horrific. The king was unable to speak or acknowledge anyone who addressed him. He seldom moved and could not walk independently. In fact, he seemed to be virtually paralysed and was barely able to hold up his own head. He just slumped in a chair or lay in bed motionless. This mysterious illness struck suddenly and totally without warning. Although it is believed that he may have suffered from a mental health condition that was inherited from his maternal grandfather, Charles V of France, the symptoms could not have been more different. Charles became violent during his bouts of illness and was said to have run through the corridors of his palace screaming. He was a threat not only to himself but to his servants and those sent to look after him. His grandson's ailment did not involve any violence or aggression. He just did nothing.

Modern historians have made various attempts to retrospectively diagnose Henry's condition. It has been described as a form of psychosis. The most common suggestion is that he suffered some form of catatonic schizophrenia. Others have suggested that the king was in fact autistic, but this does not seem a likely suggestion. There were also some troubling historical parallels: Henry's own father had died in his thirties shortly before the birth of his first child, an event which had been preceded by the loss of a major battle and the death of his brother Thomas of Clarence. Henry himself was approaching the same age and was soon to become a father himself, and then everything was compounded by the loss of Gascony and the death of Talbot. Perhaps it felt like history was repeating itself. Or perhaps the king read the events as some kind of sign. There was a story that a prophecy had been uttered of two kings named Henry: one, born at Monmouth, would rule for a short time and win much; the other, born at Windsor, would rule for a long time and lose everything. Henry VI himself had been born at Windsor, while his father was born at Monmouth Castle.

It is reasonable to suggest that Henry's breakdown in August was brought on by stress. Not only had the loss of Gascony just reached the king's ears, but he was also trying to deal with the burden of a divided realm. He had been on his way to handle a local dispute when he was struck down – the straw that broke the camel's back? – and although he was still only thirty-one years old he had recently suffered an unprecedented amount of stress and trauma. His situation would tax even the most capable ruler.

The immediate response of the government was to try to carry on as normal. At first, Henry's illness was effectively covered up and doctors were quietly summoned to help the king, who was said to be only temporarily indisposed. The treatments they meted out ranged from herbal remedies and baths to bloodletting; Henry was lucky to avoid trepanation (drilling into the skull), which was sometimes practised at this time; the council would have had to approve such an operation, and they perhaps would have considered it too extreme.

It was Queen Margaret and the Duke of Somerset who seem to have been behind the attempts to hush up the truth about the king's condition. They might not have been acting in a purely selfish manner; the political situation was already delicate, and the incapacity of the king had the potential to throw the country into turmoil. Even so, they surely wanted to protect themselves – especially Somerset, who only really had his high position due to the influence of the queen. If the news got out, their enemies could multiply in a government struggling to deal with an unprecedented situation. Kings had suddenly and unexpectedly died before: in a sense the English system was better equipped to deal with the death of a monarch than it was to deal with an adult monarch who was alive but medically unfit to rule.

By late August 1453, the royal council with Margaret and Somerset at its head was issuing orders and overseeing the day-to-day business of government. By this time Margaret would have been seven months pregnant and preparing to enter her confinement. This was a traditional practice in which a woman would retire to private apartments to await childbirth, usually with a select group of female attendants, about a month or so before her due date. Pregnancy and childbirth were difficult and dangerous in the fifteenth century and there was no guarantee that either the queen or her child would survive. Margaret entered her confinement in late September, processing to her apartments at Westminster with great pomp with her supporters Humphrey Stafford, Duke of Buckingham and the Duke of Somerset. With both king and queen out of the picture by the late autumn of 1453, most power rested with Somerset. The council was essentially an interim government now, with Somerset and allies like Buckingham at the helm.

On 17 October, the day after the feast of St Edward the Confessor, Queen Margaret gave birth to her first and only child at the Palace of Westminster. A healthy son, the tradition of the last three generations was broken by naming him Edward. He was probably named for the saint's day on which he was born because it was not a traditional Lancaster name. Finally, there was an heir to the throne and the succession was apparently secure – provided the child survived, of course. Yet the occasion was tinged with fear. Still incapacitated, the king was not present to rejoice at the birth of his son. The Duke of Buckingham carried the child to the king shortly after his birth, but the monarch barely moved and gave no indication that he knew what he was being shown. Again, this is often interpreted as a sign of Prince Edward's dubious paternity, but the king's illness was marked by virtual paralysis, so we should not read too much into the incident.

What can be observed is that the birth of her son marked a turning point in Queen Margaret's life and career. For medieval queens, the birth of a male heir was a guarantee of security. It meant that their husbands would not divorce them or dispose of them and that they were stable in their position. However, Margaret was in an unprecedented position in October 1453 as the consort of a monarch who was incapable of ruling and would be for an unknown period. Nobody could say when or if the king would recover. Parliament was due to be held in November, at which point all the interim council's best efforts to conceal the true nature of Henry's illness would come to an end; kings were expected to preside over Parliament in person.

When Parliament duly convened, events would come to a dramatic climax with factions vying for control in the absence of the king. Although the two factions are often labelled as Yorkists and Lancastrians, the terms are not contemporary and aren't necessarily accurate. Although it is true that Richard, Duke of York and those who converged around him stood against Edmund Beaufort, Duke of Somerset, who was a member of the Lancastrian royal family, things were not so black and white. Some nobles – many, in fact – sat on the fence. Several had connections with both lords, and others were reluctant to throw in their lot with either. In 1453 York was not claiming the throne, and both factions were still officially loyal subjects of Henry VI and his dynasty.

The chronicles give us a rather facetious view of what happened. Fearing that 'England would be ruined under the government of the Duke of Somerset', it claims, Parliament 'sent for the Duke of York'.[8] York's return was in fact inevitable: there was no reason to keep him away from the centre of power anymore, and doing so would only have served to antagonise him and arouse the anger of his supporters. On 23 October, when his rival Somerset was absent, he was finally summoned. Keen to maintain at least the appearance of unity in the government, Margaret was in an awkward position and could not afford to offend a figure of York's importance. When Parliament finally convened in November, the Duke of Somerset again came into conflict with his antagonist. This time, York was furious about more than the activities of his rival. He openly complained about not having been included in the council before Parliament was convened. With Somerset overseeing government, the cousin of the king and one of the greatest lords in the realm had been excluded.

York was seething. He had been excluded from the government for two years. It must be noted, however, that in the wake of the Dartford incident this was hardly surprising; the king did not exactly want a person who had skirted dangerously close to committing treason at the heart of his government. He and the queen warned York's allies to stay away from him with the implication that they would risk royal displeasure. With the king out of the picture, though, the duke was back. Parliament was soon riven by the conflict between the two implacable foes.

On 21 November, York was able to reverse royal policy with a declaration signed under the Great Seal (traditionally used only on documents approved by the monarch) that 'all men were free to serve him'. This allowed him to basically gather as many retainers around him as he wanted. On the same day, there were demands for Somerset's arrest on charges of 'treason'.

On 23 November, John Mowbray, Duke of Norfolk 'launched a blistering attack' on the Duke of Somerset in Parliament,[9] accusing him of treason and blaming him for the loss of England's lands in France. He also accused Somerset of corruption, suggesting that he had not been punished thus far because he had bribed so many people. Norfolk did not mention Somerset's known association with the queen because this would have been in poor taste. At the end of the day there could be rumours, but the wife of the anointed king was still in a position that afforded respect and few nobles would have been willing to publicly attack her or cast aspersions on her character.

Although Somerset defended himself, he was arrested and consigned to the Tower two days later. He must have had a sense of déjà vu as it was his second time there in three years, and once again he had been put there without any formal charges being laid. It has been suggested that the conflict between the two nobles had gone so far that each felt the only way to protect themselves was to try to destroy the other. The problem was that their enmity was no longer personal. Most of the nobility were linked with either York or Somerset in some way, and unless they could rise above factional loyalties there was a threat of war.

By the end of November, York and his allies had effectively wrested control of the interim government away from the Somerset. Watts argued that he may have done this by strongarming the elderly Archbishop of Canterbury and others into compliance when he launched what was effectively a coup.[10] It is worth noting that by now Richard Neville, Earl of Warwick, the son of the Earl of Salisbury and the nephew by marriage of the Duke of the York, was firmly in the Yorkist camp. This was no big surprise as Warwick had already been embroiled in a violent feud with the Duke of Somerset over lands in south Wales.[11]

It was not without cause that the queen became so concerned about the political situation that she decided to act. First, in December, she decided to try to rouse her husband. She had the Duke of Buckingham present her infant son to his father again in the vain hope that the sight of his child would be enough. Of course, it did not work. Henry barely looked up. The political situation was getting increasingly dangerous, with Parliament divided between Somerset's broadly royal faction and York's faction, and violence was erupting across the country again as nobles fell into petty feuding among themselves. Amid all this it was important to find someone to represent the middle ground, someone above partisan sympathies who could bring unity to the realm once more and represent the interests of the king and his infant son. Margaret decided that she was that person.

When Parliament reconvened in January 1454, Margaret asked to be made Regent of England.

This proved to be one of the most controversial actions of Margaret's life and reign. It earned her the censure and condemnation of her contemporaries. Even in our supposedly more enlightened age, writers have spoken of the twenty-three-year-old queen overstepping the mark. She has been accused of being greedy and power-hungry, of not respecting the kingdom's laws and customs, of insensitivity and cultural ignorance, of not knowing her place. She should have left it to her betters, who happened to be male. Yet what had she done that was so very wrong? She prepared a bill of five articles proposing the transfer of authority and kingly patronage to her.[12] Unfortunately, there aren't any records of exactly when she attempted to do this, nor more details of how. A letter recounted her presenting the bill and summarised its five articles but that is all we have – a shame, considering that this marked an attempt to become the first queen in over two centuries to be named regent. What we do know is that she wanted to rule the realm and have the power to appoint ministers like the chancellor and treasurer, as well as sheriffs and bishops.

In France, and indeed many other parts of Europe, there was a long-established tradition of female regents. The mothers of underage princes ruled on behalf of their sons, sometimes for years. Contrary to popular belief, there had also been some examples of female regents in England as well. Henry II and Stephen both elected their wives as regents while they went away campaigning or attending to matters across the Channel. The last such example came in the thirteenth century, when Henry III appointed his wife Eleanor of Provence as regent for just under a year. The title that Margaret was claiming was not necessarily unprecedented, then.

Margaret herself had direct experience of women wielding power in the absence of a man in the form of her mother and grandmother. Such a concept was entirely normal and natural to her. Also, it seemed the most logical choice when the only other viable option was the borderline treasonous Richard, Duke of York, and the government was overall in such chaos and turmoil. As the wife of the king and the mother of the heir to the throne, Margaret was the only person who could ensure that the interests and wellbeing of the Lancastrian royal family came first.

Margaret did not necessarily hate York, but she likely did not see why control of the realm should be handed over to a man who had twice tried to rebel against his king, or at least sided with rebels to that effect. Fifteenth-century concepts of loyalty were neither nuanced nor flexible. The king's personal failings did not matter; he was God's anointed leader, and opposing him in any way was potentially treasonable. York's actions had caused Margaret to mistrust him and his motives. Although he protested loyalty and had not directly struck out against her, he and her closest ally Somerset were intractable enemies and their rivalry was threatening to become deadly. If he was willing to contrive to have his enemies condemned for treason, Margaret must have wondered what else he might do. Members of the royal household were so jumpy and fearful that they placed a garrison at Windsor Castle, where Margaret was staying at the time. Something of the atmosphere of fear and paranoia that existed in London is revealed in the Paston letters when one of its correspondents warned that the Duke of Somerset 'has spies in every lord's house of this land, some posing as friars and some as shipmen'.[13]

It is easy to judge Margaret in this situation for putting her interests above those of the kingdom, but the same criticism can be levelled at both parties. While King Henry's inadequacies did have an impact on the country, there were other factors at play. Both York and Margaret were trying to protect themselves, for all the former talked about wanting to do what was best for the country. Perhaps he believed he was doing just that, and he certainly was patriotic, but enlightened self-interest was as natural then as it is now. For all he talked about Somerset and his faction harming the country, he wanted to protect himself too. York was gathering troops and supporters including Warwick and Norfolk, men who had reason to fear if Somerset was suddenly released. As Griffiths tells us, in the early months of 1453 when Queen Margaret claimed the regency the Lancastrian regime was at its most vulnerable: 'The King was helpless, his ministers frightened and confused, his magnates deeply divided.'[14]

Yet Helen Maurer has questioned this dramatic depiction of events and the degree of factionalism at play in 1453. Early in the year, Margaret had been open to hearing her friend Cecily Neville's petitions on behalf of her husband. Maurer has also traced various gifts and grants made by the queen to people affiliated with York and his allies. What was going on here? It is possible that even up to this point Margaret did not hold any personal animosity for the Duke of York. Yes, she might have been wary considering what happened at Dartford the year before, but now the Lancastrian dynasty was secure thanks to the birth of her son. York was no longer a dynastic threat, and he seems to have calmed down, brought to heel by her husband with his sacred oath at St Paul's. He had not said or done anything against the queen or her son and had professed to be a loyal subject of her husband too. Beyond this, though, it cannot be ignored that Margaret simply could not afford to alienate the greatest lords of the realm, no matter what her personal opinions might have been. She needed the goodwill of York, Warwick and his father Salisbury. It was in her best interests, and theirs, to present a united front – although York had threatened that by pursuing his feud with Somerset and his consignment once again to the Tower of London.

In this fraught atmosphere the queen was trying to break the deadlock and protect her husband and son while upholding the regime to the best of her ability. In her eyes, this meant laying claim to the authority that she needed to do this effectively. That authority was not granted. Margaret's bid to be appointed regent was unsuccessful. For all the precedents, a queen had never actually tried to claim the regency entirely of their own volition; all the other regents had been appointed to that role by their husbands. Margaret's attempt to take control may have been shocking and unexpected given she had previously presented as an unintrusive, traditional queen. Perhaps this only served to confirm existing prejudices about this suspect French queen.

A Yorkist ballad written nearly a decade after the event gives us an insight into how Margaret's claim to the regency was received by some:

Scripture says, 'Woe be to that region
Where is a king unwise or innocent.'
Moreover, it is a right great perversion
[For] a woman of a land to be a regent—
Queen Margaret, I mean, that ever has meant
To govern all England with might and power,
And to destroy the right line was her intent...

The reference to the 'right line' was a lot later, but it was nothing new to suggest that a woman holding kingly authority for an unspecified time without her husband's blessing was somehow wrong and perverse.

Had Margaret meekly rolled over and gone back to her role as the model queen after her failed bid to become regent, it is possible that all would have been forgiven and forgotten. In the short term she actually did back down, and Parliament settled the matter by appointing Richard, Duke of York as Lord Protector in March 1454. But soon after this the criticism of Margaret becomes more vicious and more personal. It is also from this point that the rumours about her having affairs and her son being illegitimate become more widespread. Why?

Margaret's career can be divided into two distinct states. For the first eight years of her reign, as we have seen, she fulfilled the typical and expected roles of a queen. In January 1453 she shocked everyone when she seemed to overstep the bounds, but there were mitigating circumstances and she basically withdrew from the public eye immediately afterwards, which is probably why the vilification did not begin immediately. It was only with hindsight that people began to measure her, claiming the regency bid as the point of no return.

Medieval English queens could wield considerable power on a domestic level, and their ability to influence the king and thereby help others must not be underestimated. What they were not supposed to do was play a direct role in politics or interfere in its mechanisms. Although some queens did so from the shadows or when working in tandem with their husband, the notion of a woman ruling independently while her husband was still alive (albeit incapacitated) was anathema.

There was another obstacle in Margaret's way which suggests that the reason she did not become regent was not necessarily personal. As regent of the realm, she would have had to 'stand above magnate rivalry and command the loyalty of all'.[15] This wasn't really true of Margaret; not because of her fondness for Somerset (as we have seen, she managed to get on with York to a point) but because of her legal and moral position as wife of Henry. Women were technically considered subordinate to their husbands in law and in religion. 'The husband is the head of the wife' was written in Scripture, and medieval people knew the Bible rather better than is often believed. In practice women could wield more authority than traditional ideas would suggest, but there were still limits. A king could not grant his decision-making power to his wife any more than God would give away his power. A woman could act as her husband's proxy or representative so long as her actions were 'construed … as expressions of his authority and will', much like the king and the clergy were the representatives of God on earth.[16] If a woman was a widow, of course, she did not have to worry about any of these things. But Margaret was not a widow. Her husband was still alive, and so she was still subordinate to him.

A man did not have any of these problems. Every man in England was technically a subject of the king, but they were regarded as having their own independent will and authority in the way that a woman did not. York's appointment as protector was based on a legal fiction that when he acted in the king's name it was as if the king himself spoke through him. Hence why some documents were authenticated with the royal signet, which was more personal that the Great Seal, during the time of Henry's illness, even though he could not possibly have applied the signet with his own hand. Margaret could only be considered to act as an *instrument* of the king's will, not someone who could wield it for him while he was still alive.

For a woman and a queen, there was yet another potential problem: if the king were to die, any man could potentially grab power by marrying her. This was one reason why so few European countries allowed for queens regnant, because there was always the possibility that some foreign prince could take power through her. In the case of a long regency, somebody with designs on the throne could potentially seize power by taking control of the person of the infant prince.

So, while Margaret may have been considered a viable candidate by some, her gender worked against her for legal and theoretical reasons. There were also certain military expectations of a lord protector, including defence of the realm, which could only be fulfilled by a man. Women could engage in warfare and combat, of course, but it was rare and generally frowned upon, especially in highborn women.

With the king failing to recover, during that eventful March there was at least one positive development when on the 15th Edward was formally proclaimed Prince of Wales, Duke of Cornwall and Earl of Chester. This move might not have entirely been due to the magnanimity of the Duke of York, however. It seems Queen Margaret was encouraged to negotiate with the council, perhaps through a series of messages. It is even possible that she arranged to release the Earl of Devon, who had been imprisoned in 1452 for his role in the Dartford incident, in exchange for her son's investiture. The six-month-old Edward was also given an allowance until he reached the age of eight, which was usually a precursor to the creation of a personal household, although of course the money went to his mother to pay for nurses and other necessities. For now, Margaret would have to content herself with that.

On 22 March, Chancellor Thomas Kemp died. This mattered because the business of the government was dependent on the chancellor, who was also the keeper of the Great Seal of the realm. In response, the government sent a deputation to the king to request advice and permission to appoint a new chancellor. They stayed for most of the day but, predictably, received no response from the monarch. A week later, the Earl of Salisbury was appointed chancellor; conveniently, he was brother-in-law of the Duke of York.

Only two days before, on 27 March, York had been made Lord Protector. The last Lord Protector had been John, Duke of Bedford in the early years of Henry's reign, and before him there had not been one for centuries. In appointing a Lord Protector, Parliament was opting for a safer, more traditional way of doing things. York decided to use his power to help his allies and to bring about some desired reforms, but he was also careful to avoid being seen as too partisan. For this reason, men from each of the 'Yorkist' and 'Lancastrian' factions were appointed to the council. Among them were William Booth, Margaret's former chancellor and now Archbishop of York; Walter Lyhart, Bishop of Norwich, who had been her confessor; John, 1st Viscount Beaumont; and Lord Scales. Although the York's brother-in-law the Earl of Salisbury was to chosen to serve as chancellor, he had also been in the king's household so it was no big shock.[17] This was clearly another attempt to create a regime which represented unity and reconciliation, and to overcome the dangerous feuds between the great men of the realm.

York was successful in putting at least a temporary end to the feud between the Percy and Neville families (naturally ruling in favour of the Nevilles) and managed to secure a reduction in the royal budget – cutting costs was always popular. However, he also tried to proceed against Somerset. The Lords were not eager to attend council, especially when York wanted to enact more controversial business. Although York was able to veto Somerset's release, he was not able to do much else because many councillors absented themselves from the proceedings against the duke. Some feigned illness, while others were a little more honest: Viscount Beaumont basically cited divided loyalties. He was the queen's man and asserted that all men should be allowed to speak their mind in council without fear of 'wrath' – in other words, without any fear of repercussions for going against the wishes of the Lord Protector. It also demonstrated York's position was only temporary and that the true and legitimate authority still lay with the royal family. Those who protested what he was doing could still align themselves with the monarch without seeming to be overeager for power or even treacherous. York did at least succeed in securing a tentative date for Somerset's trial in October 1454.

Margaret did not openly align herself with Somerset or York during the period of the Protectorate and mostly kept out of politics, though she clearly still had loyal supporters and could potentially rely on them to protect her interests in the council. Nor did York display any open hostility towards her; it was Somerset he wanted dead, not Margaret. She did not just sit around twiddling her thumbs, though. One piece of correspondence has her requesting that a Holy Relic of some kind be taken to the king, presumably in the hopes that it would lead to his miraculous recovery. That was one of only two events – the other being her son's majority – that could end York's protectorate and restore her to her previous position as consort.

It also helped that York was taken away from London in the spring of 1454, ironically by the rising tide of discontentment in the kingdom. First he had to face off an attempted uprising by his son-in-law Henry Holland, Duke of Exeter, in Yorkshire. Holland raised 200 men and found a supporter in Lord Egremont, a younger son of Henry Percy, Earl of Northumberland, who had been alienated by York's favouring of the Neville family. York dealt with this rather half-hearted rising quickly and decisively by marching to Yorkshire in person and dragging Holland out of sanctuary to be imprisoned in Pontefract Castle, but there was still a lot of resentment brimming beneath the surface. The tendency of many nobles to absent themselves from Parliament and council has already been mentioned, and suggests York did not enjoy widespread support and struggled to get things done. In addition to this, like Henry before him he was unable to find the money to pay the Calais garrison, which mutinied in response. Nor did it help that York had effectively had a peer of the realm incarcerated for months with neither trial nor charge. Such things were not acceptable; ancient laws and customs like Magna Carta were supposed to prohibit such treatment of freeborn Englishmen, even unpopular ones like the Duke of Somerset. It was a public relations disaster. If York was supposed to represent fairness, justice and the rule of law he seemed to be doing a poor job of it.

A year had now passed since Henry had fallen ill, and he showed no signs of recovery. But as autumn turned to winter there were hopeful rumours. A Londoner claimed that he had seen the new Archbishop of Canterbury, Thomas Bourchier, receive a response from the king while visiting him in his chambers. That was in late September, and no more word was heard until Christmas time. Then, all of a sudden, the queen's prayers were answered. The king recovered as quickly as he had been taken ill. He began to speak. His wife and councillors talked with him. On 27 December, the king personally sent a servant to Canterbury to give thanks at the shrine of St Thomas Becket. The queen in due course introduced him to their son, who was then fourteen months old. The royal family were joyfully reunited, with King Henry thanking God for his son. The joy prevailed throughout the capital, with processions throughout the city of London to give thanks for the king's recovery. Henry may have had his faults, and some were discontented with his rule, but he was still king and his recovery was rightfully considered worth celebrating.

In early January, the king's councillors met with him to make sure the stories were true. It was well known that York's protectorate was supposed to end either when the king recovered or his son came of age; whichever happened first. The king was now able to go back to the business of ruling, but he 'woke up to a different political reality'.[18] Kempe, his friend and trusted chancellor, was dead, Somerset was once again incarcerated in the Tower, and there was a Yorkist clique in charge of the country. It is hardly a stretch to speculate that York had little cause to rejoice at the king's recovery. Any fears he might have had were well founded. Margaret soon prevailed upon the king to release the Duke of Somerset, who was quietly removed from the Tower of London in late January, about the same time that the king went to join his wife at her favourite palace of Placentia. In early February, Somerset was formally bailed despite having already been secretly released. There was still talk of him being made to answer the charges that Norfolk had laid against him, so all was not forgiven and forgotten.

Understandably, Somerset's latest spell in the Tower had hardened his enmity towards the Duke of York and his associates. The protector had locked him up without charge for months and had apparently been preparing to have him executed without legal recourse. Very soon, that hatred spilled over into outright violence. York's first protectorate had also given Margaret cause for concern. Although York had not harmed her or really made any moves against her, he had been in a stable position and had used his power to try to destroy his main rival. She was also unhappy that she had been compelled to compromise and negotiate to extract concessions from him, even for things that were her due as queen. Who did York think he was to make the Queen of England beg for crumbs?

During the spring of 1455, the king and his wife set about reversing everything York had done during the protectorate and replacing his men with their own. Henry basically allowed it to be proclaimed that he had total trust in Somerset and did not believe the allegations against him, and then gave him free rein to do as he pleased. Furthermore, he affronted York by appointing Somerset to the position of Captain of Calais, another title York had formally held. He was letting everyone know that Somerset was back in favour and that he would go on as if nothing had changed since his breakdown. Yet things *had* changed, and irrevocably so. York had legitimately held power for nearly a year and had managed (as he saw it) to make a positive difference in the country. He had formed a triumvirate with Salisbury and his nephew the Earl of Warwick, united in their animosity towards Somerset and their desire to protect their interests.

These three men remained a force to be reckoned with, even when they were obliged to give up power. Together they commanded a large power base in the north and the

Welsh marches. Their alliance was strengthened by bonds of marriage.

By the spring of 1454, the battle lines were being drawn once again. York and his allies retreated to their estates in the north of England. The business of government continued as usual, but the air was heavy with tension. Henry seems to have noticed that the enmity between his chief lords was likely to boil over again. On 7 March, the Earl of Salisbury resigned his office as chancellor and handed it over to Thomas Bourchier, Archbishop of Canterbury, in protest after the Earl of Worcester was replaced as treasurer by the Lancastrian partisan James Ormond, Earl of Wiltshire, and the Duke of Exeter was summoned back to court. The same month, King Henry bound York, Somerset and some of their respective followers over for good behaviour. Such bonds of recognizance involved the parties making a formal agreement to keep the peace, usually sealed with the payment of a sum of money. If they failed to keep their promise, they could be summoned to court and tried, or even imprisoned for their breach of the peace. If a party failed to keep the peace, they would not get their money back. Henry was not only wielding the threat of financial punishment to keep the two lords from pursuing violence against one another, but also to encourage them towards legal arbitration instead.

York was excluded from a meeting of the royal council in April, but then he and his allies were summoned to another meeting scheduled for May. This meeting was to be held in Leicester, a safe heartland of the royal family, and was intended to bring the Yorkists to heel. They were expected to submit to the king in the presence of most of the peers of the realm, among them their political rivals. Later sources would suggest that the Duke of Somerset and the queen were plotting to eliminate York and his allies at this meeting: 'The evil Duke of Somerset ... was plotting the destruction of the noble Duke of York saying that the Duke of York wished to depose the King and rule England himself.'[19] Whether or not this was true is up for debate. In any case, York and Somerset's rivalry had turned deadly. Margaret's intentions are a little harder to discern. It is possible that she shared Somerset's concerns and feared being unable to protect him if York took power again. She may well have feared the erstwhile protector for her own reasons too, and therefore sought to weaken him.

First Battle of St Albans

When the court and the council travelled to Leicester for their scheduled meeting in May, an event took place that would go down in history as the beginning of the Wars of the Roses. It certainly changed the course of the vendettas that underpinned this period. York, Warwick and Salisbury had probably been preparing for some time, gathering troops for weeks or even months. They marched south as the royal party set off for Leicester. They spent the night at Watford, and then arrived at St Albans on 21 May. There, the king's party were intercepted by York and Salisbury, who had come with an army including 'many bannerets, knights, esquires' and others. Chroniclers say the army consisted of between 3,000 and 5,000 men.

Accounts of what happened there allow us to recreate the debacle in detail, but they are almost all told from a Yorkist perspective. Shocked at the arrival of this force, the king's lords gathered around him while the Yorkists shored themselves up 'about a crossbow shot' outside the town. From their encampment they proceeded to parley with the king, who naturally wanted to avoid bloodshed. For the better part of two days heralds were sent back and forth with letters, including one sent to Archbishop Bourchier in which they protested that they were being kept away from the royal presence and that their enemies were spreading rumours about their motives. They had come for the sole purpose of dealing with those people; they were not traitors, as York asserts in the this missive:

> We hear that there is a great rumour and wonder at our coming, and of the manner thereof, towards the most noble presence of the king, [and] many doubts and ambiguities are created in the mind of his royal majesty and amongst the people concerning our faith and duty to his highness. [Yet] neither by our coming, nor by the manner thereof, do we intend to proceed to any matter except what, with God's mercy, shall be to His pleasure, and to the honour, prosperity and welfare of our sovereign lord, his land and people...[20]

The letter took a somewhat darker turn when York asked the king to 'deliver such to us as we will accuse and they to have as they have deserved'. Basically, hand over the people whom he and his allies accused of wrongdoing so that they could mete out summary punishment. This vigilante and arbitrary approach to dealing with rivals was extremely worrying and did not sit well when taken with the Yorkists' claims to be champions of justice and good rule. The king took a hard and uncompromising line against the duke, writing, 'I shall know what traitor is so bold to array my people in my own land ... I shall destroy them.' He threatened to have anyone caught siding with York hanged, drawn and quartered.[21] The king was obviously not going to hand over his friends and chief advisors to face almost certain death at the hands of a traitor and oath-breaker, no matter what he said about his motives being pure. The Yorkists, for their part, were not going to give up and go home.

Most of the lords were present around the king on the morning of 22 May. According to the near-contemporary Dijon Relation, the Duke of Warwick's men approached the city first and blocked all the roads out. Eventually 'real fighting' began at 10 p.m., centred around the marketplace, which Warwick similarly blockaded. The English Chronicle says that the city was 'strongly barred and arrayed for defence'; in other words, the king's forces were expecting a fight. Warwick's men had to break through or circumvent these defences to enter the city via St Peter's Street.[22]

With so many confined to such a small area, the fighting would have been vicious. The king's standard fell, presumably after his standard bearer was cut down, and four members of his bodyguard were 'killed with arrows'.[23] This order of events parallels the usual strategy of late medieval English battles, which began with a volley from the archers before the hand-to-hand melée began. Henry himself was wounded in the shoulder with an arrow, but he was not the Yorkists' target and he was promptly taken to safety. Their real target was the Duke of Somerset.

After three hours of fighting, the Duke of Somerset, as well as Henry Percy, Earl of Northumberland, and John, Lord Clifford, lay dead. The Duke of Buckingham was wounded after being hit by three arrows and either escaped to the abbey or was taken there. While the Dijon Relation states that a total of two hundred men were killed, other sources suggest a far lower figure, perhaps only twenty. Partly for this reason, it is widely held that the First Battle of St Albans was not so much a battle as a skirmish designed to bring about the assassination of the Yorkists' political opponents.

Although there is some doubt over how Somerset died, it appears he went down fighting. He reportedly fled into a nearby house with some of his men but was surrounded by Yorkists who broke down the door, leaving him no choice but to emerge. He cut down four men before being felled by a blow from an axe and then hacked to death. His eldest son, Henry Beaufort, then aged about eighteen, was by his side during the fighting. He likely fought alongside his father and may well have seen him slain. Perhaps he even tried to come to his aid, for he himself was badly wounded. Clifford and Northumberland, meanwhile, were killed by the Earl of

Warwick and his men, possibly near to the blockade they had set up around the town or else near the marketplace. The battle certainly looks like a political assassination. The respective noble casualties were each cut down by their major rivals, in Northumberland's case by a member of the family he had been feuding with for decades. It was just far too convenient to be a simple twist of fate.

Although many chroniclers presented the Yorkists as the wronged and injured party, and even as the innocents, there is one account which suggests a darker side. According to the account, when the wounded Duke of Buckingham fled to sanctuary in St Albans Abbey along with the Earl of Wiltshire, a group of York's men wanted to go in and kill the two nobles. York then said that if the king did not allow him to arrest the two men, he would allow them to be slain. Buckingham was duly handed over, but Wiltshire had already fled. This is somewhat at variance with the image of a humble York kneeling before the king 'protesting that he had not opposed him but had been against the traitors to the crown' and being forgiven.[24] It sounds more like a man who was firmly in charge of the situation.

In the immediate aftermath of the battle, York and Warwick escorted the king back to London 'where they were received with great joy and solemn procession'.[25] Margaret was not at St Albans; she and her son had gone to stay at Greenwich as the king and his followers intended to travel north. Queens did not normally attend meetings of the council in person, but she may have planned to travel north to join her husband later. Perhaps the king had actually heard or at least suspected that York might try something, and so she decided to stay behind for her own safety.

Margaret would soon have heard about the events of the battle, and probably looked on as her husband marched back to London. She would most likely have been horrified at what happened to her oldest friend in England, the Duke of Somerset. When the Yorkists returned to London they engaged in damage limitation and did their utmost to bolster their own reputations. The day after the battle, Henry stayed with the Bishop of London. Two days later, he made a solemn procession to St Paul's Cathedral for the formal occasion of the crown-wearing ceremony before the court celebrated the feast of Whitsun. Some chronicles give the idea that all was rosy at this point, but there were problems beneath the surface. York and his allies were in a quandary. They now had the king in their power, but they did not dare depose him since most of the people of England were still loyal to him. Harming him would have been even more foolhardy since they had just protested their loyalty to him.

On the day that King Henry and the Yorkists returned to London in triumph, Margaret had taken refuge in the Tower of London with her infant son. This suggests a woman who was in genuine fear for her own safety and that of the heir to the throne. Considering the actions of York and his fellows this attitude was unsurprising, even if her actions were a little dramatic. After staying in the capital for the week-long Pentecost festivities, Henry and his family may have retired to Windsor Castle. His precise movements are hard to track. Michael Hicks suggests that they retreated to the seclusion of a hunting lodge near Ware. Margaret, like many ladies of the period, enjoyed hunting and was a keen rider. After the bloodshed and tumult of recent days it is no great leap to assume that the queen would have wanted her husband safely removed from the stress and trauma of domestic politics. However, there is no direct evidence of this hunting trip.

In June, York wrote to a physician by the name of Gilbert Kenner and asked him to attend the king at Windsor. We don't know what was wrong with Henry; there might have been nothing, as physicians were sometimes just summoned for general health checks. He might have been called because Henry's mental health was failing again, which would hardly have been surprising. On the other hand, the king may have been suffering the effects of his arrow to the neck he sustained at St Albans, although that was supposed to have been a minor injury. The sad irony is that Henry, having failed as a medieval warrior king on the Continent, sustained his first battle wound during an engagement fought among his own subjects on home soil.

In the summer of 1455, the recriminations began. Maurer argues that the First Battle of St Albans changed the course of events both literally and in the national psyche. It made personal the conflicts and feuds that had been plaguing the country for so long. A man close to the heart of government had essentially got away with murder. Tensions were high in the capital; people spoke of barges full of weapons being ferried back and forth. The Yorkists wanted officially to lay the blame for St Albans on the victims. However, Somerset, Clifford and Percy had all left heirs who would never be satisfied with such a position. They wanted revenge, or at least some kind of settlement or admission of guilt. They did not get it: when Parliament sat in July, the Yorkists were given an official pardon. At some point during proceedings, in the presence of the king, the Earl of Warwick and Lord Cromwell publicly argued over who had started the fighting. Knowing something of the volatile nature of the Earl of Warwick, Cromwell was visibly shaken by the encounter, so much so that he considered going into hiding with the Earl of Wiltshire. It is little wonder that the king is said to have issued an order that nobody should mention the events of the battle to him, on pain of death. His lords were arguing in his presence like impetuous children, and he had discovered that such clashes tended to come to a terrible and bloody conclusion.

By the autumn, Henry, Margaret and their son had removed to her castle at Hertford, finally leaving behind the tensions of the city and the government. Interestingly, even then York and Warwick did not leave them entirely alone. York himself went to nearby Ware, and Warwick lodged himself at Hunsdon to 'keep an eye' on the king.[26] York seems to have approved or even arranged the king's removal to Hertford, presenting it as a sort of holiday, but it has been wondered if it was actually a sort of house arrest. York staying nearby suggests he was nervous about what the king and the queen might do when left to their own devices. Perhaps he feared that they might stir up violence or even raise forces against him. On the brighter side, the castle at Hertford had previously belonged to Queen Katherine de Valois, and perhaps Henry had some pleasant memories of having spent time there with her when he was a boy.

A letter from Margaret to the keeper of the park at Ware to reserve some game for her indicates their presence around this time; it is likely that this is the correspondence that gave rise to the theory of the hunting trip right after St Albans.[27] Meanwhile, in the capital, rumours were already circulating about the king's capacity; these rumours were apparently confirmed when Henry was said to be too ill to attend the second sitting of Parliament that year in October. Dockray suggests that the king almost certainly suffered another mental breakdown. Whatever the exact the nature of his condition, in November Henry's illness resulted in York being appointed Protector of the Realm for the second time in less than two years, just under a year after he had been relieved of his duties for the first time.

Second Protectorate

York's second protectorate was as unprecedented as his first. In the first, it was noted that nobody had ever been protector for an adult monarch before. The second protectorate, however, was more controversial. The duke had effectively taken control of the king via a coup and a series of political assassinations only months before, and he had been in virtual control of the government ever since. Now that his most formidable enemies were dead, however, it could be argued that York had no real cause for grievance anymore. He'd got what he wanted, and unless he really intended to lead the country or bring about some major system of governmental reform, then his claims to represent equitable rule and to stand against 'evil councillors' meant nothing.

What York and his allies had done was unite a new generation in deadly enmity against them. They would soon be joined by some people well known at court, among them the queen. If Margaret did not personally hate York in the first half of the 1450s, she certainly did by the end of the decade. He had taken control of the realm, imprisoned and killed one of her oldest friends and allies, endangered the life of her husband, and then brought him back to his own capital as if he were a prisoner. She would tolerate it no longer. It is not without reason that this is the period in which we see Margaret begin to act openly. She discovered her political muscles, and began to truly flex them for the first time.

4

THE SHE WOLF

In February 1456, York was removed from his position as Lord Protector after a period of barely three months. The official story was that he resigned as the king had recovered enough that he was now capable of ruling independently. York had already ensured that he could not be removed without the consent of the king and the entire council.

The king formally relieved York on 25 February, around two weeks after he had arrived at Parliament with an armed escort of 300 men. Around this time, we start to see various statements in records and chronicles blaming Margaret for ousting York and asserting that she was taking control of the political arena. There is a famous line from Thomas Bocking, a correspondent of the Pastons, who described her as 'a great and strong laboured woman, for she spareth no pain to sue her things to an intent and conclusion to her utmost [power]'.[1]

It is fascinating that over the course of less than a year, in fact in the space of a few months, chroniclers and commentators went from hardly speaking of the queen at all to accusing her of usurping power and trying to take control of the entire realm. What exactly happened? Modern historians often assume that Margaret had a role in ousting York from his role as Lord Protector, and there is some evidence to back this up. However, it is just as likely that York failed to hold his position because he had so little support among the nobles of the realm. Michael Hicks has shown that only about nine lords were present at some of his great councils, most of them his allies. It is possible, though, that if York had so little support in his role, Margaret simply took advantage of her position and York's weakness. So, was Margaret personally responsible for the termination of York's second protectorate? Hicks highlights that Bocking's letter was actually written before York's protectorate was technically over, and so it is unlikely that Margaret had much to do with what happened.

York's protectorate was dominated by an issue known as resumption. This was an action, sometimes reinforced by an Act of Parliament, which required the monarch to revoke or take back grants of land, money or offices which had been given away. The idea was to shore up royal finances and allow the king to basically support himself. Of course, most nobles were opposed to this because it could threaten their interests and make a large hole in their purses. Margaret might have been the queen, but she still held certain lands and grants from the crown, and so she was probably as opposed to resumption as everyone else. It may be that she became more vocal in pleading her own case before the king to keep her servants, wards and retainers.

Resumption proved to be controversial because the king was granting exemptions to members of his retinue (and presumably those of his queen) and affinity. He was basically making exceptions to the law in order to allow favoured servants and retainers to keep what had been granted to them. It also allowed him to continue to show them favour in future.

Hicks suggests that when Bocking referred to Margaret as a 'strong laboured woman' he was saying that she 'pressed her requests to the king as vigorously as she could'.[2] These requests may have had something to do with resumption, and to grant her and her servants the exemption that they wanted. If this was the case, it might explain some of the animosity and suspicion some felt towards her. It was born of jealousy that Margaret was able to protect her rights and lands when theirs were being threatened. York's removal from office afterwards probably just seemed too coincidental.

After York's dismissal he still attended several council meetings, and Henry seems to have been keen to at least keep the duke in his good books. Margaret herself left once again for her estates in the Midlands shortly after 24 February. Her reasons can only be speculated at: some wonder if it was because she feared another coup and wanted to get herself to safety, but it may have been simply because she wanted to get away from the unhealthy conditions in London. If she did remove him from office, she did not seek any sort of revenge or punishment against him, nor did she push for her husband to send him away once again. She did, however, take steps towards moving her court to the Midlands and away from London on a more permanent basis. It might not have been due to the bad conditions in London, but rather an increasingly toxic and dangerous atmosphere. Rioting and violence were again increasing throughout the country, and in the capital things were getting more personal.

There was one person who certainly did blame Margaret for the situation in February, and that was Thomas Gascoigne, an Oxford academic and student of theology. He made a number of allegations against Margaret which originated in the air of hostility surrounding the London court. Much of it probably originated with York's great spin doctor Richard Neville, Earl of Warwick. Gascoigne had been reading Yorkist propaganda and tracts, full of accusations and insinuations old and new, blaming Margaret for the loss of France and saying that she was exerting her power and dominating the king. He was the first to openly accuse her of having pressured her husband to end York's protectorate.

Rumours even began to emerge that she was plotting to make her husband abdicate in favour of their son, and to basically rule in his stead. This may have been a hangover from her claim to the regency back in 1454, but there could have been some basis for the belief that Margaret was at the very least trying to consolidate her power.

Rather, she was trying to consolidate the king's authority and through it her own. The year 1454 had taught her that striking it out alone was unlikely to make much of a difference. Instead, she decided to wield her power through others. In late 1455, several government offices had once again been filled with men of the king's affinity. Laurence Booth became keeper of the Privy Seal; William Waynflete, Bishop of Winchester and Henry's own confessor, replaced York's relative Thomas Bourchier as chancellor; and John Talbot, Earl of Shrewsbury, son of the earl who perished at Castillon, became treasurer. Yet even here, the royal family had to be careful. Maurer suggests that they these appointments were made when the council was in session to allay any suspicions that Margaret was behind them rather than the king himself. The moves to promote resumption could well have been a response to these appointments, and the rumours about Margaret's increasing influence, while possibly arising as a reflection of the truth, soon became wildly exaggerated. If the queen was able to install men loyal to her and the king in government offices, why could she not have ensured York was dismissed as well?

The king's weakness might have made him easier to dominate, but Queen Margaret was beginning to assert herself to fill the void. Her claim to the regency had been turned down, but the new appointees would have given her increased access to the heart of the government. Although she was being careful, however, her enemies did not fail to notice this and had no hesitation in using it against her.

The Yorkist propaganda machine was in full swing, with slurs aimed at her personal life (the usual rumours of sexual misconduct) and at the legitimacy of her son, who was said to be a changeling or the product of adultery. The most creative insult, as mentioned above, was that she was planning the ultimate act of betrayal in forcing the king to abdicate in her favour. That would have been a betrayal not only of her marriage vows but of her very position and the allegiance she owed to her husband as her lord. It is unsurprising that during this period Margaret came not only to fear Richard, Duke of York and his allies but to genuinely despise them.

They were waging a war against her not with swords or polearms but gossip and rhetoric. Gradually her enemies were trying to undermine her authority by besmirching her reputation as well as the sources from which she could derive her authority, namely her husband and her son. Margaret hit back by increasing efforts to create her own court centred on herself and her son, and based in her Midlands territories. In 1457 she established her son's council; although Prince Edward was not yet four years old, this was an institution which mimicked his father's council and was meant to oversee the running of his estates, possessions and business matters such as collecting the revenues from his estates and tenants, authorising expenditures and providing advice. Of course, since Edward was barely more than a child it was really Margaret, whom he apparently referred to as 'our dearest and most beloved mother the Queen', who oversaw this.[3]

The men on this council included some unsurprising choices: Laurence Booth, William Waynflete and John Talbot. There were also Humphrey Stafford, son of the Duke of Buckingham, who was wounded at St Albans; James Butler, Earl of Wiltshire; and Margaret's chief steward, John, Viscount Beaumont. One other interesting appointment to the prince's council was Thomas, Lord Stanley, father of the Lord Stanley who would become so notorious thirty years later. Laurence Booth and his brother were both Chester men, and Stanley had at one point been justiciar of Chester. Young Edward held the title of Earl of Chester as well as Prince of Wales, and the border region was part of his lands. It is partly as a result of this that some have gone so far as to call the council an instrument in Queen Margaret's hands. All their decisions had to be rubber-stamped by her, and by carefully choosing the appointees she was able to exercise control of the localities that comprised her son's domain.[4]

Margaret also chose as Edward's attorney general Thomas Throckmorton, a lawyer with many years of experience who had worked mostly in the West Midlands. Clearly, many of her son's councillors also worked for her husband's administration in some way. It was a useful way for her to consolidate her own power and influence and to keep Henry's men in her camp. The more nobles and influential government minsters the queen could get on her side the better. In some ways the prince's council may be viewed as an extension of her own authority, and a means through which she was able to exercise rule while technically remaining subject to male authority; Ralph Griffiths tells us that 'nothing could be done without her permission.' Above all, the prince's lands were a resource which could be exploited by his parents.[5]

Notable among the councillors was the young Henry Beaufort, Duke of Somerset. If his sire had been a father figure to Margaret, who missed her own family, Henry was a close contemporary. He was eighteen or nineteen at the time of his father's death, and Margaret herself was still only twenty-five. It was only to be expected that Beaufort would be a devoted Lancastrian considering the allegiance and heritage of his family, as well as the events which befell them in the 1450s, but it was not impossible that they could lose his loyalty. Alliances were not always determined by blood or affinity; even staunch opponents could still retain affection for one another. In 1457, Margaret came up with a daring proposal to marry two of the daughters of King James II of Scotland to the Duke of Somerset's younger brothers, Thomas and John. She decided on this course of action because of rumours that James was in talks with the Duke of York and might be seeking to make an alliance with him. The situation along the Scottish border was always rather precarious, and raids or attacks were normal, but the idea of the King of Scots in alliance with a noble in his power base in the North was sufficiency worrying for Margaret to involve herself. Although the marriages fell through in the end, a truce was struck with King James in July of that year, and more importantly he was 'kept away from York'.

This event is an example of Margaret's emerging desire to dabble more openly in politics and diplomacy, to bring about an outcome which was beneficial to herself and those most reliant on her. She was still constrained by the expectations of her time, and still tended to use traditional methods such as matchmaking to achieve her aims, but not always. In October 1456, she went to the Welsh borders to negotiate a pardon for Gruffydd ap Nicholas. Nicholas was a Welsh nobleman who had been accused of various misdeeds. In 1456, he was involved in disturbances in Wales. They seem to have started when Edmund Tudor, half-brother of Henry VI, tried to 'assert royal authority' in the region. The situation quickly escalated into all-out war. The royal family were so worried about what was happening that they ordered a set of 'serpentines' – basically primitive cannons – as well as the ingredients for gunpowder while they were staying at Kenilworth.[6] Although the castle was nearly 40 miles away from the Welsh borders, and it would take an invading force the better part of a day to ride there, Henry and Margaret obviously felt the need to be prepared. It is even possible that they were gathering the weapons to launch an operation into Wales in order to deal with William Herbert, who was the leader of the forces attacking the king's men.

Herbert, another Welsh magnate and a devoted Yorkist, besieged Carmarthen Castle with 2,000 men and captured Edmund Tudor. Gruffydd ap Nicholas became involved in the hostilities, apparently on the side of William Herbert. In the end the king did not have to get involved as Herbert was eventually pacified by the forces of Jasper Tudor, Earl of Pembroke, and those involved were arrested or submitted. Margaret did not want Nicholas to throw in his lot with the Duke of York, which he might do if he felt it served his purposes. His pardon was to be given in return for his continued service and alliance to the House of Lancaster and served to stop him transferring his allegiance.[7] Later, Margaret was also involved in issuing another pardon to William Herbert, who personally offered to submit to the crown 'in return for his life and goods' (in other words, in return for not being executed or stripped of all his possessions). In Herbert's case, the charges seem to have been exaggerated to force him into submission, and one wonders if this was the case with Gruffydd ap Nicholas as well.

We can see here that Margaret was starting to take a more open role in law and justice, as well as patronage, and indirectly in politics. She was fast becoming the public face of the Lancastrian dynasty. But this was a double-edged sword. It allowed her to take real action to change at least some things, but it also drew negative attention in the form of increasingly colourful rumours and propaganda.

In politics, events were teetering on a knife edge. More and more often Margaret was choosing to stay away from London and to remain in her power base in the Midlands. York stayed mostly in his estates in Yorkshire, especially at Sandal Castle near Wakefield, although in the late summer he had to go and deal with a threat from the Scots – a threat Margaret had tried to offset with the proposed marriages to the Beaufort brothers. Another meeting of the council was held in October 1456 in which more prominent members of the government were replaced, and a 'sustained verbal attack' was launched on the Duke of York.

Henry Beaufort and the Duke of Buckingham were, as already stated, becoming very close to the queen. Decades later Polydore Vergil reported that the two dukes went to visit Margaret's court in the Midlands and convinced her that York was trying to manipulate the king with the eventual intention of deposing and killing him. Of course, it was easy for Vergil to say this with the benefit of hindsight, having known what would eventually happen. At the time, though, hostile chroniclers also suggested there was something going on, and that the nobles in question had been subject to some malign influence that caused them to turn on the duke. Margaret's decision to act in order to protect her husband is usually interpreted as evidence she ended York's second protectorate. However, not everything about the timing or execution adds up.

This has led some historians to suggest Beaufort visited Margaret in the spring of 1456, and she did not choose to act until several months after York was ousted from power, probably over the summer when he retired north to his estates and was afterwards faced with the threat from Scotland.

That summer of 1456 she travelled to Coventry with her son. When she arrived, she was greeted with a series of pageants. In the fifteenth century these were typically based on stories from the Bible or events from mythology. They were being held in this case for the feast of Corpus Christi, a festival concerning the medieval belief in transubstantiation, although it still features in the liturgical calendar of the Anglican church to this day. It is what is known as a 'moveable feast', meaning that it falls on a slightly different date each year, usually early to mid-June.

The Coventry pageant has been remarked upon because of what it can reveal about the ways in which the people of England conceived female roles and queenship, as well as how these clashed with the reality that Margaret was facing. It began with an actor in the guise of St Edward the Confessor praising the queen and her son, saying that she should pray to him if she was ever in dire straits. The connection between the eleventh-century king and her son was that young Edward was born on his feast day and was probably named after him. Edward the Confessor was not noted for his military prowess but rather for his sanctity and piety. He was a saint best suited to the inclinations and personality of King Henry VI, and perhaps not the best model for his son.

Next came a play about the nine worthies and celebrating the legendary exploits of St Margaret, the queen's namesake, who appeared in the role of an intercessor and protector. A dragon was slain, but more of the content related to the queen's role as a mother, with idealised Biblical models of motherhood and the inevitable celebration of the Virgin Mary. Margaret brought Prince Edward, at that time approaching his third birthday, along to the pageants and she would have been flattered by content referring to the prince 'in glowing terms' and celebrating her for having given birth to him. The parts comparing her husband to the great conquerors of the past such as Alexander the Great might have struck her as a little excessive.[8] She would never have said so out loud, of course.

When the king finally came to join his wife in the Midlands later that summer, and the date of another council meeting was set for October, she allegedly used the occasion to persuade her husband to change the personnel of his household in order to incorporate the sons of men who had been killed at St Albans as well as other loyalists. Thenceforth, she seems to have been more inclined to keep her husband under her close supervision. It was during this period that physical possession of the king came to be a way of establishing authority and right to rule. Whoever had the king had power.

Margaret intended to stay with her husband at Coventry, and there was talk that she intended to make it her new capital, a safe and secure power base away from London and in the heartland of Lancastrian territory. With their own court, it must have seemed like the queen was truly building a kingdom within a kingdom, a polity of her own from which she could rule. Gascoigne, the aforementioned Oxford theologian, suggested that Margaret gather her family around her so that she could 'make all the business of the realm', although the reliability of his claim is cast into doubt as he could not even get the location right (he seemed to think that the queen was based in Chester).[9] Nor was he correct in suggesting that she was personally overseeing all the business of government. This wasn't necessary. If all of the most loyal nobles of the realm were nearby and both their households were available, they could keep things ticking over. Furthermore, as Griffiths reminds us, 'the wheels of the offices of the state at Westminster could turn regardless of the king's perambulations.'[10]

The problems began when Henry stayed in the Midlands for too long. He was there for more than a year, from the summer of 1456 until late 1457. Although kings had stayed away from the capital or even out of the country for long periods before, Henry was also conducting government business from his distant residence. By the fifteenth century Westminster had been firmly established as the centre of government, so the people of London greeted the absence of the royal family and much of their court with suspicion and consternation, especially since no sessions of Parliament were held for the entire period. There were only council meetings. This action alone is what gave rise to a lot of the whispers that the queen had established her own separate government on her estates and was holding all the power in the realm. (People gossiped at their own peril; in the spring, lawyer John Halton was executed for releasing a series of 'scurrilous bills' and for alleging that the young Prince Edward was the son of neither the king nor the queen. Of course, it did not help that he had skipped bail.)

York was not excluded from any of the councils in Coventry, and in fact came and left without incident. Warwick and other Yorkist lords did not attend, but they held a considerable amount of influence over the commons. It was for this reason that London was seen as being a Yorkist stronghold. Even in this aspect, though, not everything was as it seemed. Michael Hicks has followed the paper trail and suggests that many administrative documents were still being issued in or at least signed off in Westminster. The Lord Chancellor and most of the offices dealing with the administration of government were still in Westminster, and the king seems to have been sending the papers there.

So, the entirety of the government had not *actually* transferred to the Midlands as people feared. Nonetheless, the king was the most visible representation of the government, and most people were not knowledgeable about what was going on behind the scenes.

With the royal finances based in Westminster, the king had a problem. He could raise no funds except to cover routine expenses without the assent and authorisation of Parliament or the council. The king and the queen did not have unlimited resources to spend as they wished, and seemed to have been relying mostly on the revenues raised from Margaret's dower lands and from the Prince of Wales's estates in Cheshire. Their sojourn in the Midlands didn't just separate them from the means of raising money via Parliament but also 'created obstacles to the exploitation of the crown's resources', most of which was supervised by the Exchequer. Eventually their resources would have been stretched too thin, especially given they were supporting three royals on sums intended only for the prince and his household. A return to London was essential.

The unrest and disturbances that had plagued so much of the decade came to personally involve the king. Although some feuds were dealt with, the Courtenays were still causing problems in the West Country, although some of their adherents were dealt with by Parliament. Queen Margaret came up with a novel way of bringing the family of the Earl of Devon to heel: she arranged a marriage between Thomas Courtenay, the eldest son and heir of the earl, and her cousin Margaret of Maine. She was the illegitimate daughter of Charles of Maine, her father René's older brother. As an illegitimate child – worse still, a girl – her role and future would have been undetermined and she was certainly not her father's heir, so young Margaret ended up in the English court with her cousin. Through this marriage, Margaret brought the Courtenays into the royal family, and they were later issued with a royal pardon.

Two others who faced censure for their actions in the summer of 1457 were William Herbert and Walter Devereux, an adherent of the Duke of York who had been involved in the violence in Wales in 1456. The Duke of York had appointed himself constable of the castles of Carmarthen and Aberystwyth, and after Edmund Tudor, Earl of Richmond wrested the fortresses from him, Herbert and Devereux responded by marching 2,000 soldiers into Wales. They succeeded in recapturing the two castles but they went far beyond that, capturing Edmund Tudor, who was incarcerated by Herbert for several months, eventually dying of plague in November 1456. Both were at one point consigned to the Tower of London, and Devereux was also imprisoned in the Marshalsea prison in London. Herbert proved to be more troublesome: after his initial arrest he had returned to Wales, where he 'committed further offences' and was declared to be a rebel against the crown before he eventually submitted in the May or June of 1457. Although both men were eventually pardoned, the financial penalties imposed upon them were severe.

Throughout the first half of 1457 Henry VI went on progress throughout the kingdom, attending sessions of the court and overseeing justice. During Easter he was at Hereford, and in April the Duke of York was made to surrender the constableship of Aberystwyth and Carmarthen to the second of the king's two half-brothers, Jasper Tudor, who had been created Earl of Pembroke. The duke was given the 'compensation' of £40 a year in return for the offices, but granting them to Jasper was a form of poetic justice since it had been York's men who had taken them and caused the death of Pembroke's brother. Edmund had in fact left behind a teenage wife, Lady Margaret Beaufort. Although barely thirteen years old, on 28 January 1457 she gave birth to her first and only child: a son whom she would name Henry, in honour of the king. This boy was Henry Tudor.

On or around 24 August 1457, the French attacked the port of Sandwich in Kent. The attack had been coordinated, with the army camping out on the South Downs the previous evening. Accounts vary. One says that the Seneschal of Normandy landed nearby with 3,000 men and 'took the town and pillaged it', killing several people and carrying off merchandise.[11] Of course, this event was soon exaggerated. Others later spoke of the French having destroyed the town, killing very many people. French raids on English coastal settlements actually were not that uncommon. Sandwich had been attacked before, and Southampton had been similarly raided in the fourteenth century. No matter which version of events is accurate, the town was not so helpless; although it took hours before the English were able to mount a defence, they were eventually able to drive away the French. This rout resulted in over 100 men drowning before they made it back to their ships. Although this was presented as an 'invasion', it was far from that. However, the event's impact on national morale was considerable. Most in England believed that a full-scale invasion was imminent and that the French, having driven the English out of France, were poised to try to take over England. The event was enough to bring the king back to Westminster without his queen, and a session of Parliament was finally held there in his presence in September. Parliament was clearly unsettled and frightened by what had taken place.

A grant of taxation sufficient to fund well over 1,000 archers was approved, and the Earl of Warwick, already Captain of Calais, was commissioned to defend the seas, although he really just took this as licence to harass foreign ships with impunity from his base in the last remaining English outpost in France, where he had taken up residence. Anthony Woodville, Lord Rivers was placed in charge of Rochester Castle, and Henry Beaufort, Duke of Somerset was appointed Constable of the Isle of Wight, a position he had inherited from his father.[12]

These moves to protect against foreign invaders were predictably accompanied by an upsurge in violence against 'foreigners' residing in London, the usual targets being Lombard and Flemish merchants. There were thousands in the capital, with Flemings preferring to settle in the area around Southwark, where they played a major part in the country's lucrative wool and cloth trade. The French queen may not have entirely escaped the upsurge in xenophobic sentiment, even though she had lived in England for twelve years. Of course, it did not help that the attackers were the same nationality as her, nor that she knew the man who commanded the French force that attacked Sandwich. Pierre de Brézé had once worn Margaret's colours during jousts when she was only a girl at her uncle's court. A controversial suggestion was made that the raid on Sandwich was preceded by Margaret writing to her father about the difficulties in the country. He by turn is said to have influenced King Charles VII to prepare an invasion.

Although Margaret did still have contact with her father, it is very unlikely that she was in any way responsible for what had taken place. To allow the French to attack her own people purely to show how she could command foreign support against Richard, Duke of York would have been a step too far, even for Margaret. Had a nobleman done it, it would be considered outright treason. It is far more likely that, as the Tudor chronicler Hall stated, the French attacked because they were 'much desiring to be revenged of old displeasures and great damages they had many years borne and sustained by (at the hand of) the English people', and that they simply took advantage of the turbulent political situation within the realm.[13] In this sense, Margaret could only be considered responsible insofar as she communicated with her father and complained about the situation. Perhaps she just let too much slip, and the French took advantage of that.

It was probably a good idea for Margaret to have stayed away from London in the manner that she did after her husband returned to the capital. Matters were not improving among the nobles of the realm, even if some of the feuding had come to an end. In November 1456 there had been an attempted ambush on the Earl of Warwick while he was making his way to London, and the following month the Duke of York had been attacked in Coventry by the young Duke of Somerset. Some sources say Somerset intended to murder York. Even three years after the event, the scars of the First Battle of St Albans had not faded. The sons and families of the slain had gained no redress, so perhaps this was inevitable. Nor had the factionalism in the government gone away. The problem was that the Duke of York, following the second protectorate, did not have such a strong basis for standing against the government and the king's 'evil councillors'. Instead, the queen came to represent division within the government and the realm, albeit inadvertently. In her attempts to create a strong polity that was centred around the king and those who were loyal to him, she ended up inadvertently representing a faction which was seen to be dangerously dividing the country and the government.

When the king went back to London in late 1457, Parliament again sat at Westminster and things seemed to be getting back to normal. Some historians assert that the queen herself fell back into a traditional role. The problem was that Margaret was always being made to walk a tightrope between what was acceptable and what was necessary. It might have made sense for her to do certain things that she did not end up doing, but the public would never have forgiven her if she did. She would be judged, tried, and condemned in the court of popular opinion no matter what she did. If she was too stubborn and determined – and some of her letters do suggest that – she would be branded forceful and overly harsh, far from the meek and forgiving intercessor she was expected to be.

The king had always ruled with the consent of his nobles, despite what rumours said to the contrary. As Hicks' research suggests, documents were indeed being sent back and forth, but that was not immediately obvious to most people. Even the queen could not get everything she wanted at sessions of the council, and there is some suggestion that she might have reacted by trying to move against York in some small way in the spring of 1457. Apparently, charges were read out and he was forced to swear some sort of oath, perhaps one like that which had been extracted from him after the Dartford incident in 1452. This was the same session of the council in which he had been forced to give up his Welsh castles, and around the same time several of his retainers were indicted at court sessions in Hereford.[14] Making York give up his lands and swear some kind of oath was about all that could be done.

There is no evidence that Margaret was making serious moves against the Yorkists, and she certainly doesn't appear to have been involved in a concerted effort to destroy them. However, the disturbances in the country and the continued ill feeling between the Yorkist faction and the surviving heirs of those slain at St Albans could not be ignored. The king and his leading councillors realised that what the country needed the most was unity, and so they planned to make a public show of it. What happened next has gone down in history as a laughable farce. The so-called Loveday Accord developed as a result of the unresolved tensions between the nobles that became clear at the meeting of the council which started in late 1457 and continued into 1458, with nearly every nobleman turning up flanked by a contingent of armed retainers and soldiers, in some cases hundreds. Things were so on edge that the Mayor of London and the civil authorities had to keep a close watch, going so far as to personally patrol the city and check the gates every night. They prevented at least one outbreak of violence when Lords Egremont and Clifford plotted to do away with the Earl of Warwick, who arrived late from Calais.

Throughout the next few weeks, the king seems to have held meetings privately with representatives of each of the factions. Finally, on 25 March, there was a sight to behold. Many of the great peers and nobles of the realm, including the dukes of York, Somerset and Exeter, the Earl of Salisbury and his son the Earl of Warwick as well as the queen (finally back in London), processed to St Pauls Cathedral where they attended Mass before emerging hand in hand. The queen held York's hand, and all the nobles made a show for the public, dressed in their finery with the king walking in front of them. The Loveday Accord was supposed to symbolise love, camaraderie and unity. It was a way for the great men (and one woman) to mend the rifts between them and move forward for the good of the country. A contemporary ballad described the event and the lords who appeared that day:

... love has put out malicious governance,

... In York, In Somerset as I understand,

in Warwick also is love and charity,

In Salisbury too and in Northumberland,

That every man may rejoice in concord and unity.

Egremont and Clifford, with others foresaid,

Be set in the same opinion...

The King the Queen with Lords many a one,

To worship that Virgin as they ought,

Went in procession and spared right nought,

In sight of all the commonality,

In token that love was in heart and thought,

Rejoice, England, in love and Unity[15]

In truth, this tense accord between the warring nobles had been brought about by considerable wrangling behind the scenes. All the lords were forced to enter bonds of tens of thousands of pounds, meaning they would be ruined if they broke their word. There was also a much stronger emphasis on holding the Yorkist lords accountable for what they had done three years earlier at St Albans, an event which was still looming large over the political community. Both the Yorkist lords and those who had perished during the battle were declared to be faithful liegemen of the king, effectively undermining three years of Yorkist propaganda which had presented them as evil traitors. The Duke of York was made to pay £2,000 to the widowed Duchess of Somerset, and the same amount to her son in compensation. Similarly, Warwick was made to pay around £600 in compensation to John, Lord Clifford and the three Yorkist lords founded a chantry chapel in St Albans Abbey where priests would say Masses for the slain. It was not all in one direction, however, as Thomas Percy, Lord Egremont, a younger brother of the Earl of Northumberland, agreed a ten-year truce with the Nevilles and pledged to go on pilgrimage in return for the remission of fines due to them.

There is a general perception these days that the Loveday was bound to failure from the outset, that the divisions between the lords simply ran too deep. Often the queen herself is blamed for steadfastly refusing to come to any kind of compromise with her political rivals. This does not give the full picture. Part of the problem was that by this period Margaret was seen as such a strong and dominant figure that it affected the king's credibility. As we have seen, Margaret struggled to keep her activities within the traditional remit of a woman. By 1458, it was believed that

Henry was the one acting as mediator and peacemaker. Although he was doing it for the best of reasons and had been trying to hear the grievances of each side, it was felt that he was not being sufficiently authoritative; that he was almost emasculated and was playing a woman's role. Margaret, meanwhile, was seen as the dominant one, either in opposing the Loveday on the one hand or in forcing the lords into an agreement on the other. She simply could not win.

Margaret's ally Viscount Beaumont personally escorted the Earl of Salisbury to London for the council that took place a few months before the Loveday, and even this was interpreted in the most unfavourable light for the queen. It was considered that Beaumont was Margaret's man, and that his behaviour indicated that the queen wanted all the lords to come and was exerting herself to ensure that they did so. Perhaps that was the case, but even if so, one need not interpret her as having a malicious or sinister intent. It was in her interests to promote peace and put an end to factionalism. She did not want the situation to escalate into all-out war.

It was also remarked upon that the queen arrived in London for the Loveday not in the company of her husband but with her own band of retainers, some of them armed. Considering her activities over the last couple of years – getting involved in Scotland, issuing pardons to Welsh rebels – it is sometimes argued that she 'came closer to the kingly role of stern unbending justice brought to mercy'.[16] Again, this gave rise to some colourful rumours and condemnation. One Robert Burnet said that Henry slept too long, and that he wished the king had died at St Albans. He also condemned the king for being unmanly and allowing the queen to take such an active role. It is Burnet who is the source of a story that the queen was raising solders for an expedition overseas, perhaps to France. It seems to have very little basis in fact, although it is not impossible; she did have armed men in her personal retinue.

All in all, the apparent role reversal between Henry and Margaret surrounding the Loveday was deeply offensive to contemporaries. It was considered a subversion of the natural order, and an intolerable one at that. Perhaps this was what gave rise to the idea that the Loveday Accord was doomed from the start, although this can more likely be attributed to modern historians exercising hindsight. It is generally held that the animosity between the major players was just too deeply rooted to be remedied or controlled by financial penalties and PR stunts.

5

THE BEGINNING OF SORROWS

For a few months after the Loveday there was blissful peace, and things returned to normal – as close to normal as they had ever been in that tumultuous decade, anyway. Henry even personally visited St Albans shortly afterwards, perhaps in an attempt to come to terms with the events that had taken place there. Meanwhile, jousts were held at Windsor Castle and presided over by the queen. Such pastimes had been a favourite of hers since she was a girl, and with her time given over to more enjoyable pursuits perhaps Margaret looked forward to the future with some degree of cautious optimism. By this time her son would have been about four and a half. He would have been able to speak and might even have had his own tutor.

Although the Yorkists had been pardoned for their actions at St Albans in the year the battle took place, and the pardons were upheld, the financial penalties had been relatively lenient. Moreover, the Yorkists were not held accountable for having raised an army against the king. It seems that the government did indeed make a genuine effort to ensure that all compensation which had been required by the settlement of 1458 was actually paid, to both the Yorkists and to others. Attempts were also made to raise money for the wages of the Calais garrison – an eternal problem since commanders could hardly afford to pay them out of their own pocket. The king seems to have taken pains to make sure that the Yorkist lords were included in the political process, since this had been such a problem before. The Duke of York's eldest son, Edward, when aged about sixteen, was even included in the negotiations with France that began in the autumn of 1458.

These talks were entered into in the hope of making a peace treaty with France, but plans for potential marriages were also on the table. The prospective grooms offered to French princesses included Prince Edward of Westminster, Edward, Earl of March, and the younger brothers of the Duke of Somerset. The negotiations came to include the Duke of Burgundy too. Curiously, Philip 'the Good', Duke of Burgundy had been the only person whom Henry had ever outright accused of betrayal, claiming that he wished to make war upon the duke because of the way in which he had turned against the English far back in the 1430s. In the end, the negotiations fell through, and the marriages never came about. (Although nearly a decade later, in 1468, one of York's daughters, Margaret of York, did indeed marry into the house of the dukes of Burgundy, to the son and heir of Duke Philip.)

One point of contention at this time was that Margaret of Anjou tried to have the Earl of Warwick removed from his position as Captain of Calais. Often this is read as a simple act of personal antipathy, but it was really not as simple as that. Warwick's actions were proving to be a source of real concern and controversy. The Captain of Calais was supposed to protect and defend English shipping in the Channel, but Warwick was engaging in acts of outright piracy, attacking French vessels and seizing goods, and he had no legitimate basis for doing so. This wasn't self-defence; Warwick was engaging in acts of aggression which could provoke the French into similar moves against England.

It is difficult to fully unpack what happened over the next eighteen months. All we have is a later version of events that tends to be heavily biased. However, it is usually said that the problems began with a session of the Great Council in the June of 1459. According to the pro-Yorkist English Chronicle, at this council the Yorkists were attained and stripped of all their possessions, causing them to go into open revolt. Such a story is patently unsatisfactory. Kings did not go around attainting their nobles for no good reason – well, they could, but some had been deposed for less. There would have had to have been a credible reason, and Queen Margaret's animosity towards the Yorkists would not suffice.

Trouble had apparently been brewing for months. Amy Licence has traced deliveries of weapons and other armaments for the royal arsenal to 'protect against various seditious persons'.[1] However, even this need not be taken as evidence that Margaret was planning violence against the Yorkists personally; there are various examples of armaments and weapons being gathered and armouries being stocked at various royal castles, but almost none of these were followed by action against the Yorkists. Lauren Johnson suggests that this move was brought on by whisperings of a Yorkist conspiracy, and thus was more of a defensive measure than an offensive one.[2]

Whatever the truth, there was a palpable undercurrent of suspicion and animosity when the royal family returned to the Midlands in May 1459, perhaps following another outbreak of hostilities in London. The queen, it was said, started building up her own affinity in Chester and distributing badges to various young knights and men at arms. The significance of things like livery badges is usually lost today. What they really symbolised was that a person was loyal and prepared to risk life and limb in the service of the person who had given them the badge. Margaret distributed the badge of a swan, traditionally associated with the Prince of Wales, denoting that the people who wore them were 'her' men, owing their allegiance to the queen and her son, and the implication is that she was slowly building up her own private army. These men by turn could raise their own bands of archers and other men at arms, slowly increasing the size of the force at the queen's disposal. This tendency towards building up private retinues was sometimes known as bastard feudalism, or retaining. The prince himself also started to distribute similar badges to anyone who was granted an audience with him, so he was beginning to participate in the rituals associated with kingship and lordship.

In May, a meeting of the Great Council was summoned at Coventry for June, but the Yorkist lords refused to attend. The Parliament rolls record the development:

> The Duke of Buckingham on behalf of the temporal lords sought to make the Duke of York understand how badly he had conducted himself ... and all the other lords knelt on their knees and urged you seeing the great danger to your person that ... you should no longer be pleased to show favour to the Duke of York or any others if they attempted to act against your royal estate or to the disturbance of the realm.[3]

There is some basis, then, to believe that the Yorkist lords had grounds to fear what might happen if they attended the council that June. But what brought this on? What caused such a change in attitudes in the year following the Loveday? Well, it is traditionally blamed on the animus of Margaret of Anjou, who was supposedly unable to let go of her dislike for the Yorkists. As usual, this explanation does not prove satisfactory nor credible. It is largely based on one line in a chronicle which claims that several nobles were indicted at the request of the queen. As we can see, this is not supported by the Parliament rolls, which record that the king was being warned not to show favour to those who were a threat to him.

It is possible that the Earl of Warwick may have been part of the problem. He had left for Calais in late 1458 under a cloud – possibly following an assassination attempt – while steadfastly refusing to give up his captaincy under any circumstances. After this, his father, the Earl of Salisbury, called an emergency meeting of his own personal council at Middleham Castle in Yorkshire, where it was decided that he would fully take the part of the Duke of York if there were to be problems again. He had already been on York's side, but he had not fully fallen in behind York or been wholly involved in all his actions. Now he was pledging to go all in. He was doing so in the full expectation that war might break out between the king and the Yorkist lords.

Late in the spring of 1459, Warwick returned from his self-imposed exile in Calais, where he had been serving as captain. He was given a hero's welcome, having won a naval battle against the Spanish near Flanders a few months before. But he soon began to complain about having been excluded from the king's councils, much as York had done in the past. Finally, events came to a head in June as aforementioned.

Are the Yorkist chronicles to be believed? Did the queen really seek to indict the Yorkist lords for treason? Or was it more likely the case that the queen was angry at their refusal to come to the council despite various summons, and therefore demanded that some punitive action for that transgression? The Parliament rolls seem to bear this out when they say that the earls of Warwick and Salisbury had disobeyed various summons, lied and made excuses for non-attendance while engaging in 'frivolous activities', but the real issue is that the Great Council of June 1459 is poorly documented.[4] Perhaps it was Buckingham who aggravated the issue by openly telling the king that he could not trust the Yorkist lords, using the opportunity to undermine them. Despite her personal stance, the queen does not seem to have taken such obvious actions to antagonise the Yorkists. That would have been folly, justifying any rebellion.

In the event, there was rebellion anyway. The Yorkists began arming themselves and gathering forces: the Earl of Salisbury in the north, Warwick from Calais and York from the Welsh marches where he held significant lands. In September, recent history repeated itself when the Yorkists marched upon the king, claiming once more to act in the name of the common people of the realm and against the evil councillors of the king. They had barely altered their approach in nearly a decade. The English Chronicle, with its usual stinging invective against Queen Margaret, reported that, 'dreading the malice of their enemies and especially the Queen and her company which hated him deadly', the Earl of Salisbury set off with 5,000 men to attack the king at Kenilworth. Salisbury initially intended to march south, but when the king heard of his movements he sent forces north, moving from Coventry to Nottingham. Forced to change his plans, Salisbury instead headed for Ludlow, where he intended to meet up with his son-in-law the Duke of York.[5] Queen Margaret was waiting at Eccleshall, en route to Ludlow. She had gathered nearly 800 men (depending on who you believe these forces were raised either by her or the king), who were put under the command of one of her allies, John Tuchet, Lord Audley. A veteran commander, Audley was in his early sixties and had not actually participated in combat for more than two decades. The queen was apparently not really prepared for any kind of armed conflict. Audley, however, took his own initiative and caught up with Salisbury at a place called Blore Heath, located 2 miles east of Market Drayton in Staffordshire.

St Albans notwithstanding, the Battle of Blore Heath is considered to be the opening salvo of the Wars of the Roses. On 23 September 1459, Audley arranged his forces on heathland (called a 'hedge' in the sources) with a stream nearby facing south-west. There, they waited for the Earl of Salisbury to come upon them. Salisbury saw the Lancastrian banners, and this gave him the advantage of being able to prepare to take on a larger force. One source says that Salisbury and his men tried to talk their way out of the situation, hoping to persuade Audley to let them pass. Others just say that battle was joined. What we do know is that Salisbury soundly won the battle, and that somewhere around 3,000 men on Audley's side were killed, including the man himself. However, it was something of a pyrrhic victory because two of Salisbury's sons, Thomas and John Neville, were captured.

Most of the Lancastrian casualties seem to have been sustained after Lord Audley's death and possibly as a result of being pursued by Salisbury's forces having lost the field. It is possible that as many died in the chaos of the rout as during the battle itself. One source tells us that 'many knights and squires' from Cheshire were killed, including those who had received the prince's swan livery. Elsewhere these men are described as the 'queen's gallants'. This term was not, as it would seem to modern readers, intended as a complement. The term 'gallants' was derogatory and was meant to suggest men who were of dubious moral character.

The victory at Blore Heath was cast as a victory not against the king but the queen, and a vindication of the Yorkist lords and the righteousness of their cause against her. The Brut states that the Yorkist lords realised the queen and her council ruled the entire country and that nobody dared to do anything without her permission. 'She ruled all about the King, who was a good, simple and innocent man,' it was said. The author of the Brut basically attributed the king's ability to raise troops to Margaret, suggesting nobody dared to defy her, but the chronicler probably underestimated the extent of public loyalty to the king. He had been on the throne for the better part of forty years, and despite some murmurings from certain parties, he was the only king most people had ever known.

Even if the Brut was right, and Margaret was strongly asserting herself, it is very unlikely that she was doing this for her own enrichment and aggrandizement. Almost all her actions in the last half of the 1450s seem to be defensive and protective. She took the king to the Midlands in the aftermath of St Albans, but she did not outright seek to rule the country from there; rather, they established a power base and surrounded themselves with men and women of undoubted loyalty who could be trusted to enact the royal will. When Margaret made marriage alliances it was usually with these loyal men, and issuing pardons came within the remit of the normal business of kingship.

It seems, then, that Margaret utilised her authority solely to shore up royal power and, as she saw it, protect her family. It is not impossible that at some point or another she decided that the Yorkists needed to be destroyed, but she would have considered even that to have been a defensive measure. That said, Margaret could not or would not make outright aggressive moves against the Yorkists. It is almost as if she had to wait for them to do something, and that she thought excluding them from councils might be a good way of curbing their power. Her husband did not feel the same, as is witnessed by the way in which he seems to have taken great pains to include his estranged cousin in the political process. In this regard, the king was probably making the wiser choice, and his wife seems to have respected it – even if she did so grudgingly and kept doing her own thing behind the scenes.

The Earl of Salisbury, having achieved victory at Blore Heath, continued his journey to Worcester where he joined his son-in-law York, and together they rode to Ludlow. There they spent the closing days of September waiting to see how events would pan out. Perhaps they thought it would end up like another St Albans. Perhaps they were pleased that they had dealt the queen a savage blow which had threatened her power. They knew that the main royal army was still in the field and had been heading north, and now the king (or at least his wife) was infuriated by the events at Blore Heath.

During this time, the Earl of Warwick landed in Kent and then moved through London, bringing men from the Calais garrison with him. He stopped off at his favourite residence, Warwick Castle, before joining his kinsmen at Ludlow. Altogether, they were able to accumulate an army of an estimated 20,000 to 25,000 men. Knowing that a royal army of perhaps 40,000 was moving in their direction, they headed to Worcester; it was probably easier to garrison and provision so many soldiers in the city than it was at the castle, where they would likely have been caught up in a prolonged siege. With the royal forces still bearing down upon them in October, the Yorkists were on the retreat. They continued their tried and tested tactic of pleading innocence and loyalty, claiming they only wanted to gain access to the king, but in moving an army against them the king was demonstrating that he did not believe what they had to say.

It is here, in the closing months of the 1450s, that we see Henry VI at his most assertive and formidable. He was leading an army against the recalcitrant Yorkists, not sitting helplessly as they killed his nobles or accepting their actions without question. He had forgiven them so many times and had been prepared to move on, but this time he took the initiative, building up his own army in response to rumours of the Yorkists mustering and planning to come against him. He seems to have been ready before Salisbury even set off in September.

As the king's army reached Worcester, the Duke of York decided that he was not ready to face him. He retreated once again in the direction of Tewkesbury. The meadows outside the city would be the site of the Lancastrians' last stand twelve years later, but in October 1459 they played host to the retreating Yorkists and their men. At this point, it appears that they decided to return to Ludlow. Crossing the River Severn, they finally ended up at Ludford Bridge, not far from Ludlow. When they arrived, they found that the king's army was already nearby. On 12 October, the Yorkists stopped running and prepared to fight. They dug a ditch and set up a defensive position with 'guns on carts in front of their army', anticipating that the king would be ready to engage them the following day.[6] The morale of the Yorkist soldiers was at an all-time low, especially among the men of the Calais garrison.

The explanation for what happened on the night of 12/13 October was blamed by some sources on mutinous troops; it seems that the majority of the soldiers fighting under the Yorkist lords were simply not prepared to bear arms against their countrymen and their king. Presumably sensing this, the Yorkist leaders fled in the night. The Duke of York headed for Wales with his second son Edmund, Earl of Rutland, and from there made for Ireland. His eldest son, the Earl of March, made his way to Calais with the Earl of Warwick and his father Salisbury. That same night, most of the troops of the Calais garrison who had come to England under Warwick defected to the king's forces along with their leader, Sir Anthony Trollope. Trollope's defection was enough of a propaganda coup for the king, but the disappearance of the Yorkists topped it all. With their commanders gone, the remainder of the army had little choice but to submit to the king, which they did on the morning of the 13th. The king was prepared to be merciful, and they were duly pardoned, but the same mercy was not accorded to their absent leaders.

Bolstered by the victory, the king's forces made a controversial misstep by looting the town of Ludlow (and some of the lands nearby, if sources are to be believed). Such actions were not uncommon in warfare throughout the centuries, and it need not be seen as an action which the king himself supported, let alone wanted. Some accounts, probably using a degree of hyperbole, say that the town was stripped to the walls by Lancastrian troops who had become drunk on casks of wine which they had liberated. York's wife, Cecily Neville, and his two youngest sons were found in the market square of Ludlow. One late source says that they were mistreated by the marauding Lancastrian soldiers, but this account is later and pro-Yorkist. What is known is that Cecily was given into the care of Anne, Duchess of Buckingham by Henry, who 'full humbly granted her grace' when she submitted to him.[7] Henry knew full well that the mistreatment of a duchess, regardless of her husband's actions, would have reflected very badly on him and lost him much support, so he could well have intervened to ensure her safety. Anne also happened to be Cecily's sister. Anne's husband had of course been badly injured at St Albans by York's men (some of whom reportedly threatened to murder him), so although relations between the two women were ostensibly cordial there was probably considerable tension between them. The Duke of Buckingham was also a steadfast Lancastrian, so it was small wonder that Duchess Anne treated her sister to verbal barbs and rebukes over her husband's and their brother's behaviour, and her own association with their disloyalty.

In the wake of the events at Ludford Bridge, which cannot by any standards be called a battle, the king returned once more to Coventry where he had summoned Parliament. The summons had been sent out on 9 October, before Ludford, but its proceedings were influenced by what had happened in the previous month. Attended by some sixty-six lords who comprised the vast majority of the peers of the realm, it gathered on 20 November in the chapterhouse of St Mary's Priory and was not dissolved until mid-December. This session is known as 'the Parliament of Devils' because the only real business that was carried out was the attainder and forfeiture of the Yorkists. Attainder was a legal process whereby someone was basically stripped of their legal personhood. It was the worst and most extreme penalty that could be legally enforced and was reserved for that worst of crimes, high treason. Here, in late November and early December, Richard, Duke of York, Thomas Neville, Earl of Salisbury and his son Richard Neville, Earl of Warwick were charged with treason and legally stripped of all their lands and possessions. All their actions from 1452 onwards were laid out in the Act of Attainder. The Earl of Salisbury came in for special condemnation as it was considered that his actions at Blore Heath had essentially rendered him an outlaw.

Although the writings of some contemporary authors would state otherwise, this was not easily done. It took many days for such an extreme sentence to be passed against the Yorkists, who were, it must be remembered, cousins and kinsmen to many of the higher nobles of the realm. The Act of Attainder was not 'nodded through', and the remains of two tracts that have been uncovered reveal 'protracted and agonised' debates. Little wonder, because alongside the attainder of the Yorkists there was an attempt to punish further offences, but many did not want to go in that direction. In one corner, some lords were implacable and did not think that the attainders went far enough; they even tried to move against men like Thomas, Lord Stanley, who had officially been on the Lancastrian side at the battle of Blore Heath but had failed to commit his troops to the battle. A treatise that seems to originate from the time of this parliament also hints at some of the arguments which might have been made in defence of the Yorkists' actions:

They did claim to reform wrong and extortions as they existed in this realm, yet the most endless misrule of all the world did rest in them and in their servants ... all the countries about know well what extortions, what injuries, what taking of sides and division they did and caused to be done ... and at whose occasion the King's people have been daily slain and murdered. These are notable examples of preserving the commonweal![8]

On 11 December, towards the end of the parliamentary session, all the lords and nobles were required to take an oath of allegiance to the king. This was not unusual, but what was out of the ordinary was that this time the oath included the queen and the prince as well. They were required to swear on the gospels to 'take and accept ... my lord Prince Edward, your said firstborn son, for my sovereign lord' if anything were to happen to the king.[9] These oaths were then recorded and formally sealed. In later centuries, such an action would have been highly controversial and might even have been considered treasonable as imagining the king's death. Kings did not usually require oaths to support their sons and heirs until they were on their deathbeds and wanted to secure the succession to the throne. Henry was not dying, but this oath shows the insecurity felt by the Lancastrians in the closing days of 1459.

After nearly a decade of upheaval, rebellion, violence and propaganda, this was hardly surprising. Rumours about the prince's legitimacy had reached new levels, but the prince himself was growing up. He was approaching his seventh birthday and in the medieval period that was traditionally the age at which boys would 'leave the care of women', beginning their formal education and being taught to 'understand the acts and manners of a man befitting such a prince'.[10] This was also the time when they usually began to enter adult society, become members of someone's household, learned to use weapons and were encouraged to take part in legal and administrative decisions.

The oath was designed to permanently put an end to the rumours about the prince's legitimacy by ensuring that nobody could follow through and use them as a justification for civil disobedience. The king and queen wanted to ensure the security of their dynasty, and making it so that any lords reneging on their oaths could be branded as traitors was a good way to do that. By the time the Parliament of Devils was dissolved on 20 December, in time for everyone to go home for Christmas, the Yorkists had been declared traitors and stripped of their lands, and Henry Beaufort, Duke of Somerset had been appointed as the new Captain of Calais (although he would have to dislodge the Earl of Warwick first). The message was clear: if the Yorkists ever returned to the realm they would have no lands from which to raise troops. Indeed, they would be lucky to keep their heads on their shoulders.

As the king and queen saw out the decade with their growing son, they perhaps thought that their troubles were over. Was the realm finally secure? The king may not have been pleased with what had taken place, but he had come around to the necessity of dealing harshly with the Yorkists. He surely hoped he would not have to send his cousin to the block.

The first six months of 1460 went by peacefully and largely uneventfully. Two female members of the household of Prince Edward, including his former nurse Joan Sloo, retired from royal service. However, as summer approached, rumours were heard about the Yorkists planning a return. In March 1460, the Earl of Warwick sailed from Calais to

Ireland to meet with the Duke of York. Father and eldest son were probably reunited at this time. Here they stayed for more than a month, formulating plans for their return. It was during this meeting that they may have discussed deposing King Henry VI for the first time.

Calais, which was still technically under the command of the Earl of Warwick, also remained a Yorkist stronghold and became a centre of operations. Though the Duke of Somerset made numerous attempts to dislodge him, all were unsuccessful. Most notably, in October 1459 he headed for France with a force of 1,000 men and blockaded Calais to starve out his predecessor, succeeding only in drawing the ire of the local wool merchants who relied on trade with England and the Continent. Calais was an important trading hub, and the influential merchants were losing money. They decided to throw in their lot with Warwick, and that, along with money from sympathizers in England, helped him to survive the blockade. Somerset was forced to withdraw.

Many of the remaining troops were loyal to Warwick, and much of his success is attributed to his 'superior intelligence'.[11] Warwick, it would appear, was not only a master propagandist but he also probably had his own personal spy network. As early as January 1460 a Yorkist knight by the name of John Dinham was sent to Sandwich with a force of 800 men. Once again the unhappy town was raided, this time by Englishmen, who seized several ships from a Lancastrian fleet that was being gathered there. Most embarrassingly of all, they came away with valuable hostages in Richard Woodville and his son Sir Anthony Woodville.

Invasion was expected, as revealed by the existence of various commissions of array (orders for local magnates to prepare armed forces and shore up local defences) from late 1459 and early 1460. It finally came in the June of 1460. On the 26th, the Earl of Salisbury, Warwick and York's son the Earl of March embarked from Calais and set off across the Channel. Ahead of their arrival they had sent letters and issued various seditious bills in which they denounced various lords and nobles, including the Earl of Wiltshire and Viscount Beaumont. The Yorkists made landfall at Sandwich on the same day with an army of 20,000 men.

To make matters worse, they had gained an influential new ally in the form of papal legate Francesco Coppini. He had been dispatched to England from Rome in early June and visited the royal court around 6 June, tasked with reconciling the rival factions and uniting the English aristocracy so that they would join in a Crusade against the Turks. He proved to be far from objective and detached, however, and for reasons we don't fully understand he took against Queen Margaret. It is possible that she rebuffed him or simply resented his interference in English affairs. Afterwards he ended up in Calais and came to take the side of the Yorkists. Thanks to his efforts, Warwick was able to get hold of a papal banner, a potent symbol which was traditionally carried by Crusader forces. It was an unmitigated propaganda coup for the Yorkists, suggesting they had God and the Pope on their side.

From Sandwich they marched, unopposed, to London. It got worse when the gates of the city were willingly opened to them, providing a reliable power base. How on earth did it happen that the capital so willingly accepted the return of men who had been attainted as traitors to the king? For one, the king himself had left the capital months before and by June was ensconced in Kenilworth. Secondly, Warwick had many sympathizers in London, as well as in the south-east of England. A decade before the men of Kent had been behind Jack Cade's rebellion, an event which the Yorkists had exploited to their advantage. Mostly, though, it was down to the presence of a papal legate as well as the Archbishop of Canterbury with Warwick's army, although some were also persuaded by their protestations that they were loyal subjects who simply wanted to bring about reform. The mayor and aldermen were nonetheless uncertain, requiring the Yorkists to swear an oath of loyalty.

After a decade of using the same justifications for their broken oaths, it is surprising that anyone would have taken the Yorkist earls seriously. At some point the Earl of Warwick told Coppini that the realm was ruled by the queen 'and those who defiled the King's bedchamber'.[12] This was the most blatant allegation that he had ever made. Denouncing Margaret as an adulterer in conversation with a papal legate was a serious matter. Coppini believed it, and even went on to repeat rumours that the queen was planning something nefarious, perhaps making her husband abdicate in favour of their son, whom Coppini held to be a bastard born of adultery.

Coppini then utilised the full weight of ecclesiastical authority and excommunicated the three nobles whom the Yorkists had previously denounced: the earls of Wiltshire and Shrewsbury and Viscount Beaumont. What Warwick owned in bravery and confidence he lacked in discretion. He was a little too loose tongued with the papal legate, and was reported to have called the king a 'dolt and a fool' and then to have outright stated his intentions, boasting that 'we shall drive our foes from the king's side and ourselves govern the kingdom.'[13] Nevertheless, this did not stop Coppini from writing a series of letters to the king with the intention of stopping further bloodshed, at least as he saw it. He first urged the king to listen to the petitions of the Yorkists and to enter talks with them to prevent open war, but his letters gradually took on a more frustrated and dramatic tone, warning the king of the consequences of division in the kingdom and even threatening him with divine judgement before finally saying he was not responsible for anything that happened and had done all he could to bring about a peaceful solution. Although the legate knew Henry quite well, his conspicuous Yorkist bias did not do him any favours. Nor did he seem aware that the king had been trying to reconcile the two parties and avoid open war for the better part of a decade. His response was to issue a declaration that anyone who gave aid to the Yorkist lords was to be branded as a rebel, although whether this came from him or from the queen is impossible to discern.

Buoyed by all the above, the Yorkists left London and went after the king. On 5 July they marched north. Henry heard of the army which had left London and personally prepared to lead his own troops, again in an act of assertiveness that one might not expect of this pious king. He had left Margaret in Coventry only a few days earlier. It is said that when he bade his wife farewell he told her not to join him again until she received a 'special token' that she would know had come from him. We don't know what this was, but it seems the couple had developed a means of communicating with one another surreptitiously using a sign or object which could not be easily forged or imitated by their enemies. Henry seems to have been genuinely afraid that the Yorkists would try to lure Margaret to London under false pretences. Margaret was clearly considered a force to be reckoned with by this time, and the fact that the king was worried their enemies might try to neutralise her hints at the extent of her power and influence.

Henry arrived at Northampton on 7 July and set up camp with his army. To his credit he did attempt to negotiate with the earls of Warwick and March, who had by then arrived alongside the bishops of Exeter and Ely, the Archbishop of Canterbury and an army of thousands around 10 July. He spent the better part of the morning of the 10th trying to engage in negotiations with Yorkist lords. His chief commander, the Duke of Buckingham, was reportedly so angry when the Yorkists arrived with the clergymen that he lambasted the bishops personally, saying that they 'came not as bishops' to treat for peace but as 'men of arms', and he certainly had a valid point. Chroniclers give various figures, estimating the Yorkist forces to have numbered

Above: Pont-à-Mousson, Margaret's birthplace. (Courtesy of Rolf Kral under Creative Commons 2.0)

Right: Yolande of Aragon, Margaret's influential grandmother, pictured here at her marriage to Louis II of Anjou. (Courtesy of the British Library)

Left: Margaret's father, René, Duke of Anjou. (Courtesy of the Musée d'Histoire de Marseille/Jean Pierre Dalbéra)

Below: René's home castle in Baugé. (Courtesy of Manfred Heyde under Creative Commons)

Above: Henry VI enthroned in Paris in 1431. (Courtesy of the British Library)

Right: Charles VII, King of France. Margaret's uncle and matchmaker for the wedding between Henry and Margaret.

The marriage of Henry VI and Margaret took place on 23 April 1445. (Courtesy of the Wellcome Collection)

Titchfield Abbey, site of the royal wedding. (Courtesy of John Greenough under Creative Commons 2.0)

Above: A famous depiction of Margaret, seen here seated, receiving the Shrewsbury Book from John Talbot, 1st Earl of Shrewsbury. (Courtesy of the British Library)

Right: Richard, Duke of York, who became an implacable enemy of Henry and Margaret. (Courtesy of the British Library)

Edward IV, son of Richard, Duke of York and usurper of Henry VI.

Elizabeth Woodville, wife of Edward IV.

A cross marking the site of the Battle of Towton, which saw Edward win the throne.

Louis XI, King of France and cousin of Margaret. After Towton he introduced her to her erstswhile enemy Richard Neville, Earl of Warwick, in order to plan to restore Henry to the throne. (Courtesy of the Brooklyn Museum)

The Battle of Barnet in a contemporary illustration. (Courtesy of Ghent University Library)

The decisive Battle of Tewkesbury. (Courtesy of Ghent University Library)

The execution of Edmund Beaufort, Duke of Somerset, after the Battle of Tewkesbury. (Courtesy of Ghent University Library)

Edward of Westminster, Margaret's only son. He was killed after Tewkesbury in uncertain circumstances. (Courtesy of the British Library)

Right: The Siege of London, wherein Lancastrian forces tried in vain to free Henry VI from captivity in the Tower of London a few weeks after Tewkesbury. (Courtesy of Ghent University Library)

Below: The Tower of London in a contemporary illustration. After Edward's victory was complete, Margaret was first imprisoned in the Tower.

The remains of Wallingford Castle, where Margaret was held after being moved from the Tower of London. It was run by her good friend Alice Chaucer.

The courtyard of the almshouses at Ewelme, another property of Alice Chaucer beloved of Margaret. (Author's collection)

The church of St Mary at Ewelme. (Author's collection)

The tomb of Alice Chaucer in St Mary's, Ewelme. (Author's collection)

Above: Angers Cathedral, where Margaret was buried alongside her father René and her grandmother Yolande. (Courtesy of D. Chelyadnik)

Left: Within a year of Margaret's death, Richard, Duke of Gloucester had succeeded his late brother Edward IV as king. (Courtesy of the Rijksmuseum)

On 30 October 1485, Henry Tudor defeated Richard III at Bosworth, returning the throne to the Lancastrian bloodline. The new king was Margaret's nephew by marriage and her cousin by blood.

Margaret's memory lives on today. This statue stands in the Jardin du Luxembourg in Paris, accurately depicting her defending her son Edward to the best of her ability. (Courtesy of LPLT under Creative Commons 2.0)

anywhere from 20,000 to 40,000, but they unquestionably outnumbered the king's forces. Buckingham's rebuff antagonised the Earl of Warwick, and was matched by fighting talk from the king, who said that if the earl tried to come before him he would be seized and executed as a traitor.

A little after midday, the armies clashed. The Battle of Northampton was fought in the grounds of Delapre Abbey. Although the king had a strong position, he was outnumbered, and the royal artillery was rendered useless by rain. The king himself remained in his tent and seems to have delegated the burden of command to the Duke of Buckingham. In the end, there was not much commanding to be done, and the Battle of Northampton ended up being little more than a rerun of St Albans. The Lancastrians were betrayed by Lord Grey of Ruthin, who submitted to the Yorkists without a fight, after which the men under his command helped the Yorkists reach the king's position. With shocking ruthlessness, Warwick and the young Earl of March ordered their men to spare the common soldiers but target the knights and squires. This reversal of the traditional rules of chivalric warfare was to become standard policy in the Wars of the Roses, especially for the Yorkists in later battles.

Warwick and March themselves had bigger targets in their sights. They cut down Viscount Beaumont, the king's oldest friend and advisor, as well as Thomas Percy, Lord Egremont and John Talbot, Earl of Shrewsbury. Finally, the Duke of Buckingham himself was slain while standing before the king's tent to defend his liege to the last. The unfortunate king must have heard the screams of his friends and allies as they died before the triumphant Yorkists stormed into his tent. The king, perhaps realizing that there was no escape, submitted himself to the Earl of Warwick for the second time. His sense of déjà vu would soon have been overcome by the trauma of having been witness once more to the political assassination of several of his leading nobles, whose bodies lay in the churned mud of the fields.

The monarch was once again in the hands of the Yorkists, and they marched back to the capital to await the arrival of the Duke of York. It must have seemed too easy for the Yorkists; just like last time, they had returned to England, dispatched their political rivals and seized control of the king. However, they had not reckoned with Queen Margaret. She was not going to tolerate the decimation of her family, nor the attempted ousting of her husband.

6

QUEEN RAMPANT

Four days after the Battle of Northampton, the elated Yorkists once again marched back to London with the king in tow. They escorted him back to the city with pomp and ceremony, the Earl of Warwick holding a sword aloft before the king. Unlike the last time, however, they now had no intention of submitting to another humiliating oath or taking technical control of the government while still officially submitting to the king. Although they intended to allow the monarch to retain his title, as Warwick had told Coppini, they would be the true rulers of the realm.

Queen Margaret and Prince Edward had managed to escape from Coventry, probably during or shortly after the events at Northampton. Most likely she fled once she heard of the outcome of the battle, as she and the king had already agreed that she should stay away from London at all costs. She made her way to Wales, where the pair sought refuge at Denbigh Castle.[1] The fortress dated back to the thirteenth century and was once the residence of Dafydd ap Gruffydd. It was remodelled in the fourteenth century with higher walls and a new gatehouse, but this work was incomplete. Tradition has it that Henry de Lacy, the owner of the fortress in the earth fourteenth century, wanted little to do with the place after his eldest son fell down its well to his death. Jasper Tudor had been named constable of the fortress in 1457 but had not really gained control until 1460, when he established a garrison there. It was not the safest of locations for a queen trying to stay one step ahead of her enemies, and in September she and the prince had gone to Harlech, a much more secure castle which was firmly under Lancastrian control.

Meanwhile, the Yorkists returned to the capital where they lodged the king for a time in the Bishop of London's palace before he was moved in August. They summoned Parliament to meet in October, and meanwhile they conducted business on the king's behalf and in his name. This was helped by Chancellor Waynflete handing over control of the Great Seal. With the king and the Great Seal in their possession the Yorkist lords could basically conduct the business of state with the king as their puppet. He remained 'a pliant and spiritless captive' in their hands for many months after Northampton.

During the summer of 1460, the propaganda against Margaret reached fever pitch. We have already mentioned the poison that the Earl of Warwick was dripping in the ear of the papal legate, but gossip and insinuation was rife throughout the capital city and beyond; shortly before the Yorkist force had landed a bill had been pinned to one of the city gates of Canterbury warning of false heirs, perjury and false wedlock. In this case, the 'perjury' probably referred to the breaking of marriage vows.[2] There were similar instances of handbills being distributed across the capital. These were the now commonplace allegations of sexual immorality against the queen, but they were also accompanied by allegations that the prince was not the son of the king, instead a changeling or a bastard issue of adultery. Even before the return of the Duke of York, and the momentous events which were to occur in the autumn, these were what gave rise to the rumours that the Yorkists were planning to depose the king and replace him with someone else.

By this time, the rumours were not just useful for political reasons – although that was certainly their main purpose. The social context is also interesting to examine. The accusations against Margaret in 1460 came against a backdrop of belief that rot and corruption had set in across society. England was being described in some of the more lurid verses as the realm of the devil, or at least under the control of the devil. The transgressing woman, breaking not only the laws of men but the very precepts of God himself, fit into this nicely. The fact that the woman in question happened to be the queen, the wife of the Lord's anointed, made her sins – whether actual or perceived – even more egregious. She was at the top of the social hierarchy and so her corruption was seen as an infection which could penetrate all of society. On a more practical level, there were whisperings that Margaret had an army of men from Chester ready to raid and pillage the south-east of England. Such propaganda about feared outsiders fed the anxieties and prejudices of fifteenth-century Londoners and would prove pivotal to several events in the Wars of the Roses.

Margaret would have been deeply upset if she knew what people were saying about her. It is quite probable that the rumours circulating in London and Canterbury eventually reached her at her haven in Harlech, but there was really nothing she could do about it. The only attempt at counterpropaganda by the Lancastrians was the tract called *Somniem Vigilantis*, which came out in 1459 when the Parliament of Devils was sitting. Margaret lacked the resources to defend herself with words when she was to all intents and purposes on the run. Before the printing press was introduced to England in the 1470s, handbills had to be painstakingly copied by hand. What Margaret could do, and indeed did do, was take more direct action.

In late September, the Duke of York landed in Cheshire, presumably coming from his estates in Ireland. He marched into London, as his cousin had done before him, but there was one crucial difference. He had taken on the surname Plantagenet and carried the coat of arms of his great-great-grandfather Lionel, Duke of Clarence. Although the dynasty that ruled England from 1157 to 1485 is today popularly known as the House of Plantagenet, none of its monarchs used it as a surname. Even kings were usually referred to by the place where they were born; Henry VI, for instance, was known as Henry of Windsor because he was born in Windsor Castle. Other sources say that rather than the arms of Lionel of Clarence, the Duke of York's standard bearers were carrying aloft the arms of England – rightfully carried only by the king and members of the royal family themselves. He also had a man carrying a sword aloft before him and arrived with trumpeters and great fanfare. All this is to say that he came in the manner of a king, not the Duke of York, and was carrying the royal insignia. The manner of his arrival could not have been more different to the way in which Queen Margaret and Prince Edward had journeyed out of London not long before. They had been hunted, effectively fugitives, and with few servants or attendants. One account even suggests the queen was robbed en route by one of her own servants.³ The contrast was a dramatic irony. The vanquished queen trying to find safety in what was effectively exile, the Duke of York returning to the country with great fanfare.

York had come to claim the throne itself.

He processed to Westminster Hall, where he apparently suffered his first major setback. The duke walked into the hall, up to the raised dais upon which a throne was placed when Parliament was in session, and placed a proprietary hand upon it, only to be greeted with stunned silence. He expected to be acclaimed king with cheers. He had prepared for that, even readying documents setting out his reasons for claiming the throne. He certainly did not expect such a disappointing and humiliating response. One of the lords eventually mustered the courage to ask the duke what he intended. Did he want to see the king? The real king, that is.

On 16 October, York finally made his purpose clear when he presented his claim to the throne to Parliament in the form of an annotated pedigree (what we would now call a family tree). It had become obvious that he could not just claim the throne by force. Although he might have been tempted to try, he probably wouldn't have had any support since even his friends had not been willing to acclaim him. Better to do it by legal means, allowing Parliament to decide upon the matter. Over the following two weeks in October, Parliament hedged, wrangled and agonised over making one of the most controversial decisions of the fifteenth century. York had indeed returned to England to claim the throne and had carefully set out what he believed to be his superior claim as a direct descendant of Lionel, Duke of Clarence, the second son of King Edward III. This, he argued, gave him a better claim than Henry VI and his entire dynasty, which was descended from John of Gaunt, Edward III's third son. There was one minor snag: York's claim was through not one but two female ancestors: his mother, Anne Mortimer, and Duke Lionel's only daughter, Philippa. Henry, by contrast, was descended in the direct and unbroken male line, from eldest son to eldest son, since John of Gaunt.

The proceedings in Parliament for the next two weeks were protracted and complicated. The Duke of York presented his claim to the House of Lords, and they in turn referred the matter to the king, hoping that he would be able to refute it. He, in turn, referred the matter back to them. Some have questioned whether the king was still acting as a free agent by this point or whether he was having his hand forced, but this is not certain. The recalcitrant Lords passed the hot potato of the matter of York's succession on to a small army of lawyers – and they too passed it right back. The Lords then tried to pass it on to the serjeants-at-law, a slightly lower legal authority, and they passed it back as well. Nobody wanted to deal with York's claim, but he was pressing the matter all the time. It could not simply be ignored forever.

Eventually they had to decide, and so on or around 24 October an agreement known as the Accord was finally reached. By this agreement King Henry was to be allowed to stay on the throne for the rest of his natural life. The Brut describes the decision:

> After much debate it was decreed and concluded that King Henry should reign and be king during his natural life, forasmuch as he had so long been king and was in possession. After his death, the Duke of York should be king and his heirs after him and, immediately, he should be proclaimed heir apparent and also protector of England during the king's life. if King Henry during his life broke the agreement, or any article concluded in this Parliament, he should be deposed, and the duke should take the crown and be king. All these things were enacted by the authority of Parliament.[4]

The king himself would not be deposed, but his son would never sit on the throne. The king finally signed off the

Accord, some say with a measure of compulsion or in fear that the Duke of York would kill him. Hicks tells us that there was something dubious going on and that Parliament was at this point mysteriously loaded with lords whose lands were derived through female succession, meaning they were more likely to accept the Accord, but even then it may not have had the assent of the majority. For the agreement to be formalised and for York to have proper control of the government, the king's assent was also required. This way, York and his sons were protected under the treason laws as the future heirs to the throne.

We do not know how Henry felt about his son and heir being basically disinherited. He almost certainly did not like the idea, but perhaps felt compelled to save his own skin or to simply agree to the demands that were made upon him for the protection of the realm. The pope was later to claim that Coppini might also have worked on the isolated Henry, who, given his piety, may have been more likely to listen to a man of the church.[5] If this is true, it is interesting to note that a partisan legate of the pontiff might have been behind such an unprecedented event in English history: the heir to the throne being disinherited with the approval of his own father. The consciences of many may have been assuaged by the allegations that the prince was a bastard born of adultery, and it is not hard to imagine that Coppini if present would have fuelled such rumours. Yet as Hicks tells us, rumours is all they were. There was no evidence that would have been admissible in court or accepted under English law.[6] Ergo, the prince could never legally be declared a bastard, at least not by legitimate legal process. The king did apparently try to secure the traditional lands of the Duchy of Lancaster for himself and his heirs, but this was cold comfort considering York and his sons had secured the crown, as well as the sum of 100,000 marks, which was to be drawn from the Prince of Wales's personal estates in Chester. It is hard to see this as anything other than a method by which to break the prince financially and drain his resources, weakening any later attempt to regain his birthright.

One source tells us that shortly after agreeing to the Accord on the night of 31 October, the Duke of York came and moved the king against his will from Westminster Palace to the lodgings of the Bishop of London, claiming Westminster as his property by right. Another recounts how the crown, suspended from the ceiling in Westminster Palace, crashed to the ground among the Commons as they debated York's claim. Always on the lookout for omens, the people took this as a warning of the imminent collapse of Henry's rule.

Queen Margaret, of course, would never and could never accept the Accord. It is not hard to imagine the vocal protests and possible violence that would have ensued if she had been in Westminster at the time. Maurer recounts that it was during the period of the king's captivity that she 'emerges as the leader of a genuine Lancastrian party', and it is certainly the first time that openly independent political or militaristic activities can be evidenced on her part.

At some point after the Accord was formally ratified, she held some secret meetings with several die-hard Lancastrian lords, including Henry Beaufort, Duke of Somerset, Henry Holland, Duke of Exeter, Jasper Tudor, Earl of Pembroke, and other survivors of Northampton. All of these men had been excluded from Parliament when the Accord was debated upon. Somerset and Exeter had cause to be aggrieved by what had taken place as the two men had claims to the throne. Holland was a descendant of Elizabeth, the younger sister of King Henry IV, and Somerset was a scion of the Beaufort family, the legitimised descendants of King Henry's half-brothers. All the parties seem to have agreed that they would never accept the settlement and would fight to restore the fortunes of the House of Lancaster.

Nobody is certain when or where this meeting took place, although there was some suggestion that Queen Margaret encouraged the Duke of Somerset to meet her in Hull. These talks were kept a closely guarded secret, hence the scant information we have today, but they may have taken place before the Accord was made.[7] The Lancastrians may have suspected the Duke of York expected to depose Henry, since he had made clear his designs upon the throne at the time of his return. At first there were whisperings that they planned to raise an army to recapture the king. Somerset and the Earl of Devon rode north with their forces in November or December, ostensibly to join the queen, and Jasper Tudor meanwhile recruited soldiers in Wales. Concerned by what he heard, the Duke of York felt compelled to ride north in full force to confront them. By the time it came to this, however, Margaret had vanished.

By the December of 1460, Margaret and her son had sailed from their Welsh haven to Dumfries in Scotland. Although Lancastrian nobles were gathering in the north, she does not seem to have been entirely confident that she could muster enough support to oust the Duke of York. They spent some two weeks over Christmas and New Year at Lincluden Abbey in the company of Mary of Guelders, dowager Queen of Scotland. Like Margaret, she was the mother of an underage son, the future King James III of Scotland. Margaret had come to request her help to invade England. The notion of an anointed queen petitioning the queen of another country to help get her throne back was as unusual as it was dangerous. Nothing like that had happened since the twelfth century, unless one counted the aberration that was Isabella of France, who effectively invaded England to depose her husband and put her son on the throne.

Mary was in fact a niece of Duke Philip 'the Good' of Burgundy, the man who had entered into the Treaty of Arras in 1435, practically ending the alliance between Burgundy and England. Her husband, King James II, had died only months before, famously blown up by one of his own cannon while laying siege to Roxburgh Castle on the River Tweed. Margaret wanted Mary's help, or more correctly wanted to enter a treaty with her: a guarantee of Scotland's neutrality if she made an attempt to march an army into England to recapture her husband and restore him to the throne. She may have made various agreements, including a possible arrangement to marry young Prince Edward to one of King James's daughters, but one particular condition was far more dangerous. Margaret is reported to have made an agreement to cede the city of Berwick-upon-Tweed to Scotland.

There were of course parallels with the cession of Maine more than a decade earlier, which had cast such a shadow over Margaret's marriage. Yet a treaty with Scotland was of such importance to Queen Margaret that she was willing to agree to something which would have been unthinkable to most of her subjects and a terrible affront to national pride. James II had been raiding over the English border for years, and the idea of the queen making any kind of alliance with the enemy of England sullied her already tattered reputation. However, if the Scots chose to capitalise on the instability south of the border they could destroy any attempt Margaret might make to gather an army and march south unmolested. She was short of allies, with the Burgundians leaning towards the Yorkist camp and the King of France having fallen out with the Pope, whose legate was also in the Yorkist camp, so she was prepared to go to greater lengths in order to ensure success. She did not think of the long-term consequences, and this was to prove disastrous.

Margaret finally marched south in the opening days of 1461. By that time, she had received news of a great victory. In the closing days of the previous year, a force of Lancastrians had decisively defeated York and Salisbury. The former had ridden north to deal with a rebellion stirred up by the dukes of Somerset, Exeter and Northumberland as well as a few other lords. He then retired to his fortress at Sandal Castle in Yorkshire for the Christmas season along with his second son Edmund, Earl of Rutland and his brother-in-law Salisbury. When they arrived around 21 December, the castle turned out to be poorly provisioned. For some reason, on 30 December, they left the safety of the castle. It is possible that they left on a foraging expedition, perhaps to hunt the plentiful game in the surrounding woodland, but it is widely held that they were lured out through deception. In the fields and meadows near to the castle there lurked a large Lancastrian force, probably under the leadership of Somerset and Lord Clifford.

Sometime in the evening, the Yorkists 'found themselves trapped in narrow fields' some miles from the castle.[8] It has the feel of an ambush. The Yorkists were soundly defeated in the ensuing skirmish, with Edmund, Earl of Rutland killed. Contrary to Shakespeare's later depiction of events, he was not a young child in the care of his tutor but a boy in his late teens, perhaps seventeen. Thomas Neville, a son of the Earl of Salisbury, was also killed, along with up to 2,000 others at what would be known as the Battle of Wakefield. There may be some truth in the idea that Neville was killed by Lord Clifford, possibly while fleeing from the site of the battle, in an act of revenge; Clifford's own father had been cut down at St Albans.

Wakefield was more than just a battle, it was an opportunity for the major families of the realm to settle scores. The Earl of Salisbury was taken alive and was later transported to Pontefract Castle as an honourable prisoner of the Duke of Somerset. Although one or two sources say that the Duke of York died during the battle itself, tradition states that he was in fact taken captive and executed or killed shortly afterwards. Most say that he was humiliated and mistreated by the Lancastrians, who mocked him for trying to claim the throne. A famous story recounted in the usually pro-Yorkist Whethamsted's Register says that he was treated in a manner akin to that faced by Christ before his crucifixion, with a crown made of paper (or possibly reeds) put on his head, and his enemies pretending to pay obeisance to him and beating him before he was beheaded. This was probably an attempt to make York look like a martyr and should be taken with a proverbial pinch of salt.

York and his son the Earl of Rutland were dead. One of Salisbury's sons was killed as well, although the earl himself was spared, perhaps because he had argued against some of York's activities and the treatment of the king. This did not save him for long, however. It was reported that the following day he was set upon at Pontefract Castle and beheaded. The culprits were said to have been common men, although one chronicle has it that a man known as the Bastard of Exeter was behind the execution. This could refer to an Exeter man born outside wedlock but it could also mean someone associated with the Duke of Exeter. Michael Hicks tells us that the execution was masterminded by one William Plumpton, a gentleman from Yorkshire.

Over the last five centuries, a legend has developed that Margaret of Anjou was present at the Battle of Wakefield and was personally involved with the death of the Duke of York. Of course, the most famous depiction of this was in Shakespeare's *Henry VI, Part 2*, in which Margaret is shown stabbing the duke after tormenting him with a handkerchief stained with the blood of his son, Edmund. However, it was not just the sixteenth-century playwright who accepted this version of events. Some modern and early modern biographers did as well, and it has become the currency of novelists. Yet there is no truth in this story. Margaret was still in Scotland when the battle took place, although she would have soon heard of the outcome, and she returned to England shortly afterwards.

By the time of the battle, England was not only dividing into factions but also splitting along regional lines. London, the south, and the Midlands were Yorkist strongholds, but the north, much of Wales and the West Country were effectively under Lancastrian control. Margaret returned to a realm where most of the nobles did not support the Accord, at least not in theory. Despite that, it had still been passed, demonstrating that what the nobility wanted and what was passed were two different things, and that they could essentially be strongarmed into doing what they were told. Moreover, they may have accepted that the last decade of Henry's reign had been beset by almost constant conflict and turmoil. Although deposing an anointed king was considered anathema to most, some may have wondered if it was for the best. Perhaps it would be good to have a ruler who could bring more stability to the realm.

By 5 January the queen had hammered out an agreement with Mary of Guelders and returned south with her son to discuss the matter with her council. Margaret was therefore 'presiding over a rival shadowy government at York with its own council and minutes'.⁹ By 20 January she had announced the alliance with Scotland, and her council had approved it – although one wonders if they were aware of the full nature of the negotiations, particularly the agreement to surrender Berwick-upon-Tweed.

After the deaths of the Duke of York and the Earl of Salisbury, Margaret probably planned to return the realm to the state it had been in before the Accord. King Henry would sit on the throne, and her son would be established once more as the Prince of Wales. It was not to be. The year of 1461 became known as the Year of Battles, with no fewer than three fought on English soil (some say four). The first came soon after the queen's return. The Yorkist faction was now effectively led by the Earl of Warwick and Edward, Earl of March. Despite the deaths of their leaders in the opening days of the year, the determined Yorkists still had two things in their favour: they were in possession of the king and in control of the capital.

The victory at Wakefield did have one more ironic consequence: it caused the papal legate to rethink his loyalties. Coppini began writing to the queen to refute allegations of his Yorkist sympathies (which were obvious), fervently protesting his loyalty. In one letter, he claimed he would rather be flayed alive than betray the queen. He reassured her 'that we love and revere [the queen] as much as any man living, she herself knows, and she has seen and experienced that we did not abandon her when she was in difficulties, and for her cause and wellbeing we are ready to suffer anything in this world'.[10] Eventually the legate would return to Rome, where his unwarranted interference in English affairs did not go unnoticed. He was eventually stripped of his position and replaced.

In early February 1461, an atmosphere of fear and anxiety pervaded throughout southern England. The Crowland Chronicle spoke of the queen riding north, accompanied by a large army of Scotsmen and rough northerners. He referred to them as a 'whirlwind from the north' and coloured his narrative with lurid details, comparing them to a plague of locusts devastating the land with their appetite for plunder and wanton violence. According to him they were set to 'overrun the whole of England' with the 'impulse of their fury'. He detailed all their supposed atrocities, including robbing churches and cutting down helpless clerics who got in their way.[11] Before long, it was not just the anonymous monk behind this part of the Crowland Chronicle who was repeating the stories of a great and terrible army of northerners and Scots heading south. It was also reported by Clement Paston, a member of the prominent Paston family, in a letter to his brother that 'the people of the north rob and steal' and had been allowed to threaten the goods and livelihoods of everyone in the south of England.[12] These more lurid stories are almost definitely false. B. M. Cron identified some of the places Margaret's army are supposed to have ravaged and destroyed; there is no evidence whatsoever for wholesale destruction, nor of concerted attacks on churches and civilians. Some observers were not even clear on which areas had been ravaged and just gave generalised reports which are not backed up up by later evidence.[13]

Yet the claims were believed, and people accepted them without proof, feeding into the narrative that the queen planned to wreak her vengeance by sacking the whole of southern England. Yorkist propaganda in early 1461 was therefore predictably focussed on stirring up fear of the queen and her army of evil foreigners hell bent on destruction and mayhem. It was imperative that Margaret did not return to London with a huge army and widespread support. It is of course worth noting, however, that although the more graphic stories can be put down to propaganda and social prejudice, there might have been some grain of truth in them. Considering the difficult conditions over that winter, it was inevitable that some pillaging, 'petty theft and illicit foraging' would have taken place. As in any marching army of the time, there may have been problems enforcing discipline.[14]

Another suggestion is that the stories had their basis in the actions of the Earl of Northumberland, who took to raiding and ravaging the lands of the Duke of York. Yet Margaret was in no way responsible for the actions of the Earl of Northumberland, and since York was an attained traitor the earl's actions may have been seen as legitimate. Either way, all the above only served to play into the hands of the Yorkists and to justify the animosity that people generally felt towards northerners and Queen Margaret. Indeed, the presence of Scots was even worse as far as the xenophobic English public were concerned. However, many of the troops in the Lancastrian armies were Welsh, with leaders from the Midlands and even the West Country.

It was in this context that the Yorkists decided to go on the offensive. Edward, Earl of March had spent the winter at Gloucester and was determined to stop Jasper Tudor from leaving his base in Wales to join the queen's forces. Together they could have formed a large and formidable force, perhaps an unstoppable one. On 2 February, having moved from Hereford to cut off Tudor's route into England, the Earl of March stopped near a site called Mortimer's Cross. About 17 miles from the city, it straddled a crossroads near the River Lugg. There he engaged a small Lancastrian army consisting of many Welsh troopers and men from the border country under the command of both Jasper Tudor and his father, Owen Tudor.

Although the armies on both sides seem to have been relatively small when compared with some of the other battles of this period, Mortimer's Cross is most famous for the meteorological phenomenon known as a parhelion which preceded the battle. This occurs when a patch of bright light appears on one or both sides of the setting or rising sun so that it looks as if there are multiple suns in the sky. It is usually the result of sunlight being refracted or split by ice particles in the air. A double parhelion occurred in the frozen winter morning before the Battle of Mortimer's Cross. March and his men, looking on, saw three suns rising on the horizon. Some took it as an ill omen, but he reacted quickly to cheer his men, claiming that the three suns represented the Holy Trinity of the father, the son and the Holy Spirit, assuring them it was a sign of divine favour. More than a century later, Shakespeare would have March interpreting it in a very different way, seeing the 'three suns' as representing the three surviving sons of the Duke of York: himself, middle brother George and youngest Richard. It symbolised the upcoming victory of the House of York and the change of dynasty.

The battle itself is a poorly documented affair, but it seems to have been relatively short and ended with a resounding victory for the Yorkists led by the Earl of March, Lord Audley, William Herbert and Sir Walter Devereux, the latter having been involved in a rebellion some years before. Owen Tudor's division tried to attack the Yorkist flank but was repelled and the entire army broke and ran. Although most of the leaders escaped, the English Chronicle relates that around 4,000 Welshmen were killed, and Owen Tudor was taken captive. Perhaps angered at Jasper Tudor and his allies like Wiltshire evading capture, March had the sixty-something Owen Tudor executed in the market square at Hereford shortly after the battle. Alternatively, he might have been following what was becoming standard policy in the Wars of the Roses by dispatching captured enemy leaders rather than sparing them or ransoming them. The Lancastrians had done as much at Wakefield, although it seems to have been ultimately started by York and his Neville allies at St Albans.

On 12 February, the unfortunate Henry was placed on a horse and taken out of London in the midst of a Yorkist army led by Warwick. The host headed north, intending to confront the main body of Queen Margaret's army as she approached the capital. It must have been truly a remarkable sight to behold: a King of England in the hands of his enemies, bundled onto a horse and forced to ride out against an army led by his queen. Not a queen who was intending to depose him, as Isabella of France had done over a century before, but a queen still loyal to him. A queen who wanted to see him restored to power as ruler in his own right and reinstate their son to his rightful place in the succession and commence ruling alongside them.

Henry may well still have been agonizing over the loss of yet another of his relatives, this time his stepfather Owen Tudor. Although he did not know him nearly as well as Jasper did, Owen was still the man who had married his mother when she had been a widow for year, and he had rewarded him with lands and estates. Now he was being dragged hither and thither, put on display by the men who had deposed him. Perhaps Henry had simply given up and meekly submitted. After all the trauma of the recent years, alongside the illness which had caused the crisis of 1453, it is not unlikely that he had suffered a complete breakdown. This may have compelled him to avoid conflict and suffering, making him seem pliable and willing to concede to whatever was asked of him. Although there were times in his reign when he asserted himself (usually at the instigation of others), Henry does seem to have been naturally eager to please others, and this side of him was probably more visible in the turbulent events of the 1450s.

Warwick took King Henry with him as a figurehead in the hopes of preventing Queen Margaret's army from attacking them, and perhaps to provide a veneer of royal authority. In doing so he could level charges of treason – and the threat of execution – at anyone who marched against his army. He created a strong fortified position to the north-east of St Albans, as well as an outpost in Dunstable. He also posted a division of archers near the centre of St Albans to block progress through the town itself. Margaret's army did indeed move towards St Albans, and came up against Warwick's archers as he anticipated. The rain of arrows forced them back to the western edge of the city, where the main armies finally met at a place called Barnet Heath.

It is hard to ascertain the exact size of the two forces. One chronicle estimates the Yorkist army to have numbered as many as 100,000 men composed mainly of the commons of England. The idea here is that all the commons turned out to fight for the cause of reform and good government against the wicked queen, but it is doubtful that the army was so large. Another chronicle makes an interesting reference to Burgundians among the Yorkist ranks. These men used handguns, a new and largely untried technology in England. Warwick had gained Burgundian support during his time as Captain of Calais, but his overreliance on his new technology and foreign soldiers may have proved a disadvantage in the end. The Lancastrians attacked Warwick's position by scaling a hill, and bad intelligence told him that they were several miles away when they were actually attacking. He also did not realise they had taken Dunstable in a night-time assault some hours before. Warwick's left flank broke following the daring uphill charge and was routed. Some suggested that his mounted pikemen and handgunners got in the way and prevented the rest of his troops from properly engaging with the Lancastrians. Another source said that they had no stomach for the fight. This reliance on foreign mercenaries or levies was to become a common feature in the Wars of the Roses, but they often proved to be a burden, owing no loyalty to their commanders and lacking emotional investment in the outcome. After the left flank fell, the centre and right quickly followed.

Warwick's army abandoned the field, the Lancastrians winning the day in a monumental victory. King Henry was found and reunited with his wife and his son for the first time in more than six months. However, in the aftermath of the battle there was an unsavoury episode that was used to criticise the queen and her son. Lord William Bonville and Sir Thomas Kyriell had been appointed by Warwick to act as bodyguards and escort the king. Both were former Lancastrians who had defected to the Yorkist ranks, but they had refused to leave their posts and flee with the rest of the Yorkist forces. Perhaps they hoped that they could change sides again. They were badly mistaken. The two were executed shortly after the battle, officially at the behest of the Prince of Wales. The idea that the seven-year-old prince ordered their deaths is taken by most historians as evidence of a violent and bloodthirsty streak in the child, proof positive that he was some kind of evil psychopath. It was reported – by the Yorkists at least – that King Henry had promised the men would be pardoned and that Margaret simply ignored this because she was vindictive. Recently, this perspective has been revised. The loyalty of Kyriell and Bonville was clearly suspect, and they were not the only such high-status men who had defected, abandoning their oaths of fealty to the anointed king and joining with a man whom many still considered a traitor. Lord Wenlock, once the chamberlain of Queen Margaret herself, had also defected to the Yorkists. She probably felt more keenly the betrayal of men who had previously been loyal to her person than those like York, who had never served her.

It is likely that the queen wanted Kyriell and Bonville executed but had her son officially pronounce the sentences. Why? Johnson explains that it was because the prince 'would be exposed to the harsh realities of kingship far earlier than Henry had been', which included his role as 'arbiter of royal justice'.[15] This does make sense: in the space of one year he had gone from being the Prince of Wales and heir to the throne to an exile stripped of his lands and inheritance, wandering the realm with his mother seeking allies wherever they could be found. Now he was at the head of an army retaking the throne for his father. He'd had to grow up fast, and he may have been inured to dramatic and traumatic events by that time.

Lancastrian actions after St Albans have also been convincingly demonstrated to have been more political than personal. Margaret and the king allowed two of the captured Yorkist leaders, Lord Berners and Lord Montagu, to escape with their lives. Minor members of the Neville and Beaumont families, they'd fought with Warwick's army but were merely imprisoned. This was not the horrible bloodletting that marked so many other battles of the period. B. M. Cron recounted how Edward, Earl of March had ten men executed following his victory at Mortimer's Cross, including Owen Tudor as already mentioned. Tudor, in his sixties, was no direct military or political threat to Edward, unlike Bonville could have been to Henry and Margaret. Owen was also a loyal subject fighting in the service of his king, having never changed sides, unlike Bonville and Kyriell. It does look as though March, not Margaret, was the one who was being vindictive in 1460.[16]

The Lancastrians had won the Second Battle of St Albans, but they most assuredly had not ended the conflict. Warwick escaped and joined March once more. To achieve the final victory, the king and queen had to retake the capital, but that was to prove easier said than done. The Lancastrians are often said to have failed in their campaign in early 1461 because they failed to consolidate their victory at St Albans and delayed their march to London. But why did they delay?

The main reason was that rumours of a pillaging northern army had made the people of London reluctant to admit Margaret and her forces. The mayor is alleged to have written to Margaret shortly after the battle, promising to allow then into the city on condition that they did not pillage or plunder the city. She promised as much, but it is claimed she did not punish those in her ranks who had been plundering in other parts of the country already. Also, the mayor was not as free to act as he thought. The people were frightened, and they might riot if he went against their wishes. For the next few days, delegations were sent back and forth from the city to the royal family. One of the first delegations consisted entirely of noblewomen, including Anne, Duchess of Buckingham and Jacquetta of Luxembourg, Dowager Duchess of Bedford.[17] They went specifically to the queen, leading to the suggestion that she was effectively in charge of the army and was dictating strategy and policy. The king seems to have been a mere passenger while they pleaded with the queen not to bring into the capital an army that might do violence upon its citizens. The wealthy and powerful city corporation members were the ones who had to be persuaded. They, along with the aldermen, were the movers and shakers of fifteenth-century London.

Margaret's assurances were not trusted, nor were her continual protestations that she meant no harm to London or its citizens. Although she does seem to have been making some progress with the mayor and the leading men of the corporations, the commons were unmoved. Yorkist propaganda about rampaging northerners bent on destruction had found purchase among the people of the capital and they were incensed at the idea of Margaret's troops entering the city. Also, personal rumours about her conduct and personality had reached fever pitch and there may have been genuine hatred of the queen by this time. Meanwhile, she was struggling to control her men, who were hungry and had not been paid. There was a real risk that they could begin foraging again – which usually turned into pillaging – and in doing so break her promise. She had been able to broker a deal with the Mayor of London to send supplies, which would at least have staved off hunger, but a mob erupted in violence and attacked the supply wagons full of provisions before they left the city. Increasingly desperate, Margaret sent a small force of knights to Aldgate demanding entry, and another to Westminster. Both were repelled.[18]

The queen's situation was becoming increasingly desperate when, in late February, it was rumoured that March was on his way to London with a massive army. This time there was no talk of loyalty to the king or removing evil councillors. He intended to claim the throne in his own right. In the preceding weeks, he and Warwick had already been spreading it abroad that they were entitled to take the throne because the king and the Lancastrians had breached the terms of the Act of Accord. No longer was Edward required to wait until the king was dead to claim what he believed was his rightful inheritance.

By the end of February, Margaret had to make a choice. She split her army, which was now threatening mutiny due to lack of pay and provisions. She divided the army in two and sent one division back to Dunstable. Eventually, she and the king retreated to the north of England having been unable to gain entrance to the capital. It was a devastating blow. The king and queen had effectively lost the support and control of their own capital city. But perhaps Margaret hoped that by keeping control of her troops she had done something to dispel the rumours and would be able to return to the capital later, with her soldiers reprovisioned and rested.

Yet worse was to come. Soon after Margaret's departure, Edward, Earl of March entered London. Unlike the Lancastrians, he was welcomed into the city. The Yorkists had long been more popular among the common people, at least in London, than with the nobles and peers of the realm. This was mostly due to Richard, Duke of York's reputation as a reformer and a champion of the common people who wanted to bring about just and equitable rule. Regardless of the truth of this image, it struck a chord with the common people who had grown tired of a weak and ineffectual king whose rule was blighted with violence and unrest, and whose apparently immoral, sinful and treacherous she-wolf of a queen was seen to be the power behind the throne.

On 1 March, the Yorkists issued a formal proclamation saying that Henry had forfeited his right to the throne by breaking the terms of the Act of Accord. George Neville, Archbishop of Exeter and brother to the Earl of Warwick, gathered a group of men at Clerkenwell, and there he set out the Earl of March's claim to the throne, asking the men present whether they thought Henry was still fit to be king. 'Nay,' they cried. When asked if they wanted the Earl of March as their king, there came a resounding 'Yes'. Three or four days later, this impromptu ceremony was repeated when Edward rode from his lodgings at nearby Baynard's

Castle with an escort of around 5,000 men. When he appeared, 'a great crowd' of common folk alongside the lords of the realm acclaimed him as the man they wanted to be king. A stirring sermon setting out his claim was delivered at St Paul's Cathedral by none other than Bishop George Neville.

In what looks like a carefully managed spectacle, Edward graciously accepted the people's offer of kingship and progressed to Westminster, where a sort of coronation ceremony was enacted. He knelt before the Archbishop of Canterbury and the rest of the lords present and solemnly swore to 'truly and justly keep the realm and uphold its laws'.[19] They responded by dressing him in royal robes, and then processed with him to Westminster Abbey, where he was offered St Edward the Confessor's sceptre, part of the traditional coronation regalia, before entering. If the account in the London Chronicle was anything to judge by, this was a far from ordinary coronation for a medieval English king, and Edward's claim was at this point largely based on the right of acclamation. Nevertheless, he emerged as King Edward IV. Although Edward himself later dated his own reign from 4 March, he had yet to solidify his claim to the throne. He had taken the throne only because Henry VI was absent and his noble supporters had managed to get the commoners to support his claim. They wanted Edward as king, but an informal coronation ceremony organised by a faction did not a king make. Edward therefore set out to prove his right to rule in a tried and time-honoured manner.

By battle.

7

QUEEN IN EXILE

Edward had checkmated the Lancastrians, who now retreated north with their army. Nobody was expecting the son of the Duke of York to have himself proclaimed king, except perhaps the relatives who conspired with him in the closing days of February to make it happen. He had entered London with a small, effective and disciplined division of troops, and above all he was popular with the people. Although his coronation and his response to being 'offered' the throne was obviously stage-managed, and many of those behind it were hardcore Yorkists, Edward already had a lot going for him. Despite being only eighteen years old, he was extremely tall, athletic and good looking. He promised a new hope for the realm.

This contrasted sharply with the popular view of Henry and Margaret, at least in the capital and insofar as the surviving sources allow us to determine it. Henry was by this time considered weak and ineffectual, barely fit to rule the realm, and his wife was seen as the true power behind the throne: forceful, vicious, with little regard for codes of honour and the good of the realm. Of course, sentiment in London did not represent the entirety of the country, but it was important because it was the centre of government. There could never, of course, be two kings; one had to go, had to be deposed or, better still, killed. The war was no longer a matter of simply restoring Henry to the throne by getting him back to London. The Lancastrians were now fighting for their very survival, and so were the Yorkists. If Edward IV had been defeated in battle in the weeks after his 'coronation' he would have been a mere footnote in history, a usurper and pretender who presumed to claim the throne but was soon crushed by the rightful ruler. Of course, this did not happen.

Henry, on the other hand, could no longer raise troops and rally them to his cause on the grounds of their loyalty to him as monarch now that someone else had proclaimed themselves king. Of course, Edward's claim to kingship was not suddenly and automatically accepted in the entire country. Those who were already dissatisfied with Henry might rally to him, as well as men from his own lands and estates, but he had only been on the throne for weeks. There were many who were still loyal to Henry.

Edward began gathering troops to his cause almost as soon as he was crowned, and before the end of March 1461 he had built up a large army. Rather than waiting for the Lancastrians to make another attempt on the capital, he took the initiative and went after them. Edward had, according to ambassadors present in London, stated a desire to exterminate King Henry and his line as revenge for what had been done to his father. Such sentiments were difficult to reconcile with the culturally Christian background of the time period, but medieval kings were expected to wage war and punish evildoers, and from his point of view this accurately described Henry and his queen.

Dealing with Henry had also become an imperative due to rumours circulating that Margaret's father, René, was gathering an army and planning to invade England to come to the aid of his daughter. He was apparently even seeking the assistance of King Charles of France in this endeavour. Edward would not be able to survive a combined French invasion as well as a war against the Lancastrians in the north.

In hindsight, there actually may have been some truth in these rumours. A letter from February 1461 exists from Pierre de Brézé to the King of France in which it becomes clear that Queen Margaret had been sending envoys to France and was in regular communication with both the king and Brézé by means of a go-between by the name of Maurice Doucereau. Brézé wanted to know King Charles's intentions towards his niece. More revealingly, he mentioned that all correspondence and communication should be treated with the utmost secrecy, as this extract reveals:

Writing to the queen, except by way of Doucereau, is neither possible nor reasonable, for if one wrote, and the letters were intercepted, no other procedure would be necessary in order to put her to death. For those who are with her and on her side knew her intention, and what she has done, they would unite with the others to put her to death ... considering the personage [involved], it is not appropriate to put the matter into so many hands. And I beseech you, Sire, that no one ... see this letter, nor what the said Doucereau will show you, because of the danger which could ensue for your said niece, which would be very disagreeable.[1]

We do not know the nature of Margaret's 'intention' as mentioned in that letter, but her long-time friend Brezé clearly thought her life would be at risk if it were discovered. There is a good chance that she was considering major concessions in return for military aid from her uncle in France, perhaps even surrendering what little territory England still held. She was prepared to go to such lengths to restore her husband to his throne.

We have to assume that Edward IV had some idea of this when he marched north with his army a few days after his coronation. We do not know the exact size of the Yorkist forces, especially since they were effectively split into three separate contingents under different commanders. Edward and his own troops marched from London. Then there was a force raised by the Earl of Warwick from his own estates and the West Country. Finally there was Warwick's uncle Lord Fauconberg, who came with his own troops. Fauconberg was a younger brother of the Earl of Salisbury and a member of the vast Neville family. By the end of the month the host had reached Yorkshire, each respective division converging at an unknown location having journeyed separately.

Edward had a total of eight peers fighting for him, with those previously mentioned bolstered by John Mowbray, Duke of Norfolk and John de la Pole, Earl of Suffolk. Pole was the son and heir of William de la Pole, who had been beheaded on the boat during Jack Cade's rebellion over a decade before, but unlike his father he proved to be a staunch Yorkist. He would only have been in his late teens at this time, but the Yorkists had cemented his allegiance through marriage to Edward IV's sister Elizabeth. The Yorkist army, now mustered near York under their various leaders, encountered a small division of Lancastrians under the command of Lord Clifford and John, Lord Neville at Ferrybridge near Pontefract on 28 March. They were there repairing the bridge in a vulnerable position when Warwick came upon them and routed them.[2] Although Ferrybridge is usually considered a small skirmish and an easy win, it was not without cost. Some chroniclers estimate that as many as 3,000 men died, and Warwick as well as his second-in-command sustained injuries. Edward's main force caught up with Warwick's later in the day, and eventually pursued the Lancastrians, who had by then begun to flee. Lord Clifford himself was slain during the rout, an arrow to the throat generally said to be the cause.[3]

The following day, 29 March, was Palm Sunday. In the Christian calendar, this marks an important part of the Easter Season, commemorating the day when Christ had ridden into Jerusalem on a donkey and been hailed as the Messiah by crowds waving palm leaves. That morning, Edward's army met with Henry's main force at a place called Towton, about 15 miles away from York. Most of the peers of the realm had turned out in favour of Henry and were present at the site or close by, showing that he still had much support among the nobility. He had been on the throne for the best part of forty years, longer than most of them had been alive or could remember, and they were all bound to him by oaths of fealty. Such oaths were not easily broken.

Some put the size of the two combined armies gathered at Towton as high as 100,000. This is huge even by the standards of later centuries, but at the time it was even more impressive, equating to nearly 2 per cent of the total population of England. Although the numbers may not have been that high, it is known that the Yorkists were outnumbered by the Lancastrians who had been 'deployed on a plateau of agricultural land' abutted by a river called the Cock Beck.[4] Battles fought near rivers seldom ended well, and Towton was no exception. The Yorkist force had one major advantage from the outset, and that was morale. Edward's men were still frightened, but he personally walked up and down his lines and gave a rousing speech saying he would live or die alongside them in his cause. Henry, meanwhile, did not lead his army; neither he nor Margaret were even present at Towton. They were at York awaiting the outcome, leaving their commanders and nobles to fight the battle for them. Margaret perhaps did not want to risk Henry being captured again if the battle went badly, but her decision to stay away deprived the Lancastrian troops of an important rallying point.

Battle was joined in the midst of a snowstorm. It was hard for troops to see far in front of them, and movement would have been difficult. Such adverse weather conditions became common during the battles of the Wars of the Roses, especially those involving Edward IV, and gave rise to rumours of supernatural intervention. This battle, like many others, began with volleys of arrows before descending into a brutal melée. For many hours men hacked away at one another in 'a sore and long and unkindly fight'. Bishop George Neville said that the battle lasted from sunrise to late at night, and another said that it lasted the best part of ten hours. It was the bloodiest battle ever fought on English soil, and if the sources can be taken seriously then it was also one of the longest. Furthermore, it was a resounding victory for Edward IV and the House of York.

Sometime after midday, when the two armies had been at a stalemate for hours, a cry of victory went up for the House of York as reinforcements arrived under the Duke of Norfolk. This new wave of men convinced the Lancastrian troops to finally break and run. Soldiers who had not perished in the battle died during the rout; many were drowned in the frantic dash across the Cock Beck. According to a newsletter printed a week later, some 28,000 died just in the battle, not counting those who drowned while fleeing. This is a greater toll than in any battle fought on British soil before or since, and more even than during any single day of the Battle of the Somme. Among the dead were the Earl of Northumberland and his brother Lord Egremont as well as the Earl of Westmoreland, Viscount Beaumont, Lord John Neville and Sir Andrew Trollope, the man who had commanded the Lancastrian forces at the Second Battle of St Albans.

Mass burial pits have been uncovered near the site of the battle. Corpses there bear wounds which some modern historians have interpreted to suggest a massacre after the fight was won. This atrocity may well have been committed by men in a frenzy of bloodlust after hours of killing, as the majority of the dead seem to have been common soldiers instead of nobles or knights who would usually have been captured.[5] Years later, a chantry chapel was built near the site of the battle where priests said prayers for the souls of the many thousands of dead on both sides.

Before night fell on 29 March, Henry and Margaret had heard about the outcome of the battle and fled from their refuge in York. They went north with only a few servants, first to Newcastle and then on to Scotland. Henry was now a fugitive in the kingdom he had ruled for his entire life. It must have seemed that God himself had turned his face away from him. Victory in battle was often interpreted as a sign of divine favour, and Edward's magnificent victory at Towton was explained by most of the people who mattered as a divine vindication of his claim to the throne. This was confirmed by the wild celebrations that greeted Edward upon his victorious return to London, after which he was treated to a proper coronation ceremony at St Paul's

Cathedral. Another event which followed closely on the heels of Edward's official coronation was the execution of the earls of Devon and Wiltshire, who had both been captured at Towton. Here was a grisly display of Edward's newfound authority; he could execute anyone who fought against him, even though their only crime had been to side with their king. A round of attainders followed, with most of the surviving Lancastrian lords being formally deprived of their lands and titles.

At the beginning of April, the exiled Lancastrian royal family arrived in Scotland. Henry was lodged at Linlithgow Palace, where Margaret had previously stayed while on the run. It must have been a strange and perhaps humiliating thought to realise that he was now a guest in the very same palace where his wife had stayed while pleading for Scottish assistance. The queen and the prince were nevertheless welcomed back to Scotland by Mary of Guelders and treated as honoured guests, eventually staying with her at Falkland Palace in Fife. The palace was extensively remodelled and rebuilt in the sixteenth century, when it became one of the favourite residences of Scottish monarchs, but in the fifteenth century it had yet to reach its heyday.

Margaret had struck up something of a friendship with the dowager Queen of Scotland. Their circumstances were similar: two mothers to young sons, one a widow and the other married to a man who was barely alive for long periods of time. Although Towton had ended in defeat, it was largely due to Margaret's efforts that the Lancastrian royal family had even survived to reach that point. As

Wolffe has mentioned, most kings who were deposed ended up being killed soon afterwards. Indeed, Margaret had probably insisted on staying at distant York to avoid her husband and her son facing the same fate.[6] The protracted nature of the battle had also given them time to escape north before the Yorkists could find them. The best the vengeful Yorkists could do in the end was attaint Henry and behead two captured nobles. As long as Henry, and more importantly his son, were still alive, then Edward IV would never really be secure on the throne.

Interestingly, Edward IV had Margaret attainted at the same time as her husband, during the first parliament of his reign in November 1461. It was highly unusual for women to be attainted for treason alongside their husbands, or even in their own right. In 1459, Alice Montagu, Countess of Salisbury had been the only woman attainted because she refused to submit to the king's mercy and had apparently fled abroad with her husband or her son, the Earl of Warwick.[7] Two years later, the Yorkists imposed the same legal penalty on the entire Lancastrian royal family. Around the same time, Milanese ambassador Prospero de Camulio, who was staying at the English court, reported gossip that Margaret was planning to poison her husband and to take up with the Duke of Somerset before coming to reclaim the throne for her son. This was a natural progression from the stories about her sexual misconduct which had been circulating for years. If she was capable of throwing morals to the wind and cheating on her husband, why not do away with the hapless Henry as well? It is curious that the attainder passed against Margaret in the November parliament referred to Edward of Westminster as 'her son', and it is no coincidence that this is around the time when we first hear the story about Henry claiming the boy had been conceived of the Holy Spirit.[8] Even though Henry had been deposed, it was still necessary to try to discredit him and thereby legitimise the actions of Edward IV.

Margaret began plotting to regain her husband's throne almost straightaway. Fortunately, she was not without supporters in England. Several Lancastrian nobles were still alive, although some kept their heads down and seemed to throw in their lot with the new king. The Yorkists were able to establish their power over most of the Midlands, the West Country, and the south as a result of the decimation of the aristocracy at Towton, but the castles of Bamburgh, Alnwick and Dunstanburgh remained Lancastrian strongholds for now. On the other hand, almost all of Wales was subdued by the Yorkists within a year of Towton, save for Harlech Castle, which remained the sole Lancastrian outpost under the command of the irascible Jasper Tudor.

Margaret may well have asked once more for Scottish aid, and her adversaries at least believed that she got it. Disturbances in Northumberland in July 1461 were blamed on Henry. They may simply have been the kind of border raids all too common in the region, but the raiders were very likely aware that their queen mother was entertaining the Queen of England, and she was a French queen to boot. France and Scotland had long been allies. Maybe they felt aggrieved on her behalf and took it as an opportunity to attack England. By July, Margaret was already communicating with supporters in England. She sent her two steadfast partisans Robert Hungerford, Lord Moleyns and Sir Robert Whittingham as envoys to France, and separately sent Henry Beaufort, Duke of Somerset to the Burgundian court. They were sent with letters for her uncle, King Charles, in the hopes of making a truce to allow Henry and Margaret to take refuge in France if doing so became necessary.

Margaret's plans went awry on 22 July 1461, when King Charles passed away. He was succeeded by his son Louis, who became King Louis XI. Long estranged from his father, Louis had been living in the Burgundian court for some years. The sudden and abrupt change in the political situation, as well as a series of misunderstandings, resulted in the arrest of Hungerford and Somerset and the confiscation of the papers that they were carrying.[9] They were not released or allowed to have an audience with King Louis until October of that year. The other problem was that King Louis had long been associated with the Burgundians, and the Burgundians were allied with the Yorkists. So, Somerset and the others returned home with only a few empty promises from Margaret's cousin. Edward IV had sent envoys to France himself in October, and they had enjoyed a warmer welcome as well as more success.

Finally in August there was reportedly a Lancastrian attempt to take over Carlisle, which ended in miserable failure. The fluctuations in political power throughout Europe enabled the Yorkists to gain the ear of the new King of France, and added to the cacophony of voices demanding that the Scottish queen hand over her guests as false traitors to the new King of England. Since Mary of Guelders did not hold a great deal of political power – and even that was waning – this did not happen, even though concerted pressure was put upon their host. By the close of 1461, Margaret was running short of allies. She had to act.

In February 1462, she decided to take matters into her own hands and embarked for France, landing in Brittany on Good Friday. It was the first time she had set foot in her home country for seventeen years. She had left as a child to be wed; she returned as a thirty-one-year-old queen whose husband had lost his throne and whose family were living as exiles in a foreign kingdom.

Yet she had not lost hope. Margaret did not come alone; she brought her son Edward with her. He was eight years old by April 1462, and got to meet his grandfather René of Anjou, who was at that time present at the royal court for the first time. René was Edward of Westminster's only surviving grandparent. Margaret's mother Isabel had died when she was still pregnant with him, and his paternal grandparents had died years before the boy was born. Henry V hadn't lived to see his son's first birthday, but it seemed as if young Edward of Westminster was destined to take after his famous grandsire, not his hapless father Henry VI.

Margaret went to see King Louis herself to make an alliance with him and gain his assistance in placing her husband back on the throne. As usual, this came with a cost, and the price that Margaret was prepared to pay was Calais. Or at least that is what is usually argued. In fact, the agreement that Margaret was prepared to make was not as simple as giving up Calais in return for French military assistance or selling it. Calais was still in the hands of the Earl of Warwick, and the agreement Margaret wanted to make was that if the city could be wrested from Yorkist control it would be put under the command of another lieutenant for the period of a year. In that time, Henry would raise money to pay back a loan of 20,000 pounds. If he could not repay the loan, then and only then would the city be handed over. Calais was essentially being put up as collateral for a loan of money which Margaret hoped to get from the King of France.

Margaret's plan worked. She secured the financial and military assistance she wanted in the form of forty-three ships and eight hundred soldiers as well as a peace treaty with France. The soldiers were put under the command of her old friend Pierre de Brézé.

Despite this initial success, however, 1462 was to be a year plagued with misfortune for Margaret. In the month of her landing in France, Aubrey de Vere, Earl of Oxford and one of his sons were sent to the block for having allegedly corresponded with her and conspired with her to plan a landing in Essex. This demonstrated that Edward was prepared to brutally suppress all opposition to his rule, especially from those who might seek to undermine it. That was his right as king, but it showed that even communicating with Margaret carried great risk.

When she returned to Scotland with the troops and ships, she picked up Henry and together they landed near Bamburgh. With such a small force (probably numbering no more than a couple thousand), the Lancastrians only really managed to recapture the castles of Alnwick, Bamburgh and Dunstanburgh, replacing the garrison at Alnwick, before Margaret was forced to withdraw to her haven in Scotland with about half her troops. Disaster struck when her ships were wrecked in a storm off the Northumberland coast, resulting in the capture of most of her troops on Lindisfarne. Margaret and Henry themselves barely escaped and had to make their way back to Berwick with their tails between their legs.[10]

In the end, the attempted military campaign of 1462 was a resounding and costly failure, and the Yorkists managed to undo what little was achieved by laying siege to Alnwick Castle and eventually recapturing it. But why did the plan fail so miserably? One reason was the double dealing of the allies upon whom Margaret relied. In the summer of 1462, Mary of Guelders made a peace treaty with the Yorkists which threatened to deprive Henry and Margaret of their sanctuary and of any future Scottish military assistance. The treaty only lasted a couple of months, and before it even ended the Earl of Angus strove to deprive Margaret of her political influence and power. Mary, like Margaret, was a woman in an unfortunate position, and her attempts to get involved in domestic politics backfired badly. Angus, like the Yorkists in England, used allegations of sexual immorality to destroy her reputation. Margaret had therefore been prevented from recruiting more troops from Scotland, meaning she and her largely French forces had been forced to wait in the three castles for local nobles to join them. By that time it was late October, and either because of a lack of support or the adverse winter conditions, nobody arrived to support Margaret and her invasion did not take place. In the end, hearing Edward IV was sending troops up to meet her, Margaret had to flee.[11]

John Paston estimated that Edward came north with an army of up to 20,000 men to retake the three northern castles and to deal with Margaret over the winter and spring of 1462/3. At Christmas, Dunstanburgh and Bamburgh fell, although Edward was willing to be merciful and allow the Lancastrian leaders to submit. Henry Beaufort, Duke of Somerset was one of those leaders, and when he obliged Margaret was deprived of one of her most important commanders and allies. Even Jasper Tudor was allowed to leave unmolested and return to Wales. This departure from Edward's more ruthless behaviour in previous years was probably due to the rumours of a huge Scottish army preparing to come over the border; it would not do to alienate military men who could come in handy if they were to unite against a larger threat. Also, Edward's short reign had already been plagued with plots, conspiracies and political unrest, and he was beginning to realise his position was not secure. It seemed wise to show mercy, especially towards important members of the old regime, with the hopes of reconciling them to his rule and hopefully winning their loyalty.[12]

Return to France

By January 1463 only Alnwick remained under Lancastrian control, and even that was under siege. Brézé and another long-time Lancastrian ally, the Earl of Angus, attempted to relieve it, but this venture too ended in failure, and the castle eventually fell to Yorkist control permanently. By the spring of 1463 two years had elapsed since Henry had lost his throne, and Margaret had achieved next to nothing. Her forces had been massively outnumbered and outgunned in 1462, and support from the local nobility and gentry had not been forthcoming.

Another invasion attempt was launched in May 1463 when Margaret crossed the border with Lancastrian forces once more. This time, they had their sights set on another castle in Northumberland: Norham Castle, just 7 miles from Berwick-upon-Tweed. Norham was constructed in the twelfth century to defend a ford over the River Tweed, and its strategic importance was so great that it was fought over by the English and Scots for centuries; it was besieged no fewer than thirteen times. Henry and Margaret took their forces to Norham with two other noteworthy companions, Mary of Guelders and the young James III of Scotland. Back in 1461 there had been rumours that the Scots planned to attack Norham, and Margaret had handed control of nearby Berwick-upon-Tweed back to them in 1460, as well as offering her son in marriage to a Scottish princess in a desperate bid to secure Scottish support before the campaign which culminated in victory at the Second Battle of St Albans.[13] Now the Scottish royals accompanied her because she had promised to let them keep Norham if they succeeded in taking it.

Edward IV responded in a timely manner, dispatching the Earl of Warwick and his brother John Neville, Lord Montagu. After a siege that lasted eighteen days the Nevilles routed and scattered the Lancastrian and Scottish forces. Margaret and Henry once again escaped and fled back north. A short time later, a story began to circulate about how Margaret and her son were set upon by violent thieves who stole her jewels and were poised to slit their victims' throats when the two managed to give their attackers the slip and escape into a forest. They were soon set upon by yet another thief, however, at which point Margaret dropped to her knees and begged their attacker to spare 'the son of your king'. Once again (or so it was said), Margaret's pleading worked, and this thief helped them safely find their way out of the forest and reunite with Henry and the rest of their party.[14]

The Lancastrian royal party limped back to Scotland in late July, but it soon became apparent that refuge there was not assured. The rout at Norham had effectively destroyed Margaret's last hope of a combined Scottish and Lancastrian invasion. Considering how Mary had made a treaty with the Yorkists in 1462 and how the allegiances of her cousin the King of France and the Duke of Burgundy seemed to change so quickly, it had surely become apparent that her circumstances were precarious. Scotland was no longer safe, and she could no longer rely on military support, especially when it was given based on promises she might not be able to keep.

In the closing days of July 1463, Margaret set off for France along with her son, some remaining members of her household and a few loyal nobles, probably including John Courtenay, younger brother of the Earl of Devon. Although none of them knew it, this was to be the last time that Margaret and young Edward would ever see Henry. On 3 August, she landed at Sluys in Flanders. This seems a strange choice since it was part of the lands of the Duke of Burgundy, whose sympathies were quite firmly Yorkist. Her intention was to try to sway the duke in the hopes that he would make no permanent or binding alliance with Edward IV, who had dispatched an embassy to St Omer in late July. It was led by George Neville, Bishop of Exeter. Margaret left her son in Bruges and personally rode to St Pol near Dunkirk, such was her dedication to the cause. According to tradition, Margaret travelled in disguise dressed as a poor woman. Although this is not proven, if true it might indicate that there also was some truth to the stories about her having been accosted by robbers on previous occasions. If she travelled in the clothes of a poor woman, it meant she didn't want to stand out, and probably didn't bring with her anything worth stealing because she didn't want to be attacked again.

When she reached St Pol, her tenacity at last paid dividends. She was received cordially by Philip, Duke of Burgundy and given money and fine clothes, but received only empty promises as far as the conflict in England and any dealings with the Yorkists were concerned. Philip essentially patted her on the head and sent her on her way. By October, he had made an alliance with Edward IV and promised to give no more aid to Henry. He made a similar alliance with France, and then, just to make up the unbeatable prile of three, he also made an alliance with Scotland. In August 1483 both Mary of Guelders and the Earl of Angus died, so the alliance was made by James Kennedy, Bishop of St Andrews, who had previously been a friend to the exiled English royals. This raised the very serious possibility that Henry could be extradited from Scotland at Edward IV's request, and with both France and Burgundy sworn not to offer any assistance the family were no longer safe.

It was probably for this reason that Margaret decided not to return to Britain in 1463 after meeting Philip of Burgundy. Instead, she headed east and threw herself on the mercy of the only person that she felt she could still trust: her father. René of Anjou was alive and well, and he was just about the only person willing to offer a place of safety to Margaret and her son.

8

THE WHEEL OF FORTUNE

Over the autumn of 1453, Margaret settled at Koeur Castle in the Duchy of Bar. Bar was situated in Lorraine, a region of France which shares a border with the modern countries of Germany, Belgium and Switzerland. Part of France today, it was then within the Holy Roman Empire. It was also part of René of Anjou's extensive holdings and was the birthplace of Margaret's mother. No castle of the name survives in the region today, but it became Margaret's home for seven years, from the autumn of 1463 until summer 1470.

Margaret lived there with a few select servants and certain nobles who had chosen to join her, and they formed a sort of court in exile. Among the individuals who resided at Koeur with Margaret was Sir John Fortescue, a former Chief Justice of the King's Bench who also served as King Henry's unofficial chancellor. He was tutor to Prince Edward both before and after his father was deposed. He wrote a book entitled *The Laws and Governance of England* in the 1450s or the 1460s. This treatise was written for the instruction of the young Edward, who studied it during his time in exile with his mother. His education was badly disrupted due to the events in England, but thanks to Fortescue he did not miss out on learning about all matters relating to government and law. There was also a poet by the name of George Ashby present at Koeur, who wrote a poetic treatise for Edward entitled *The Active Policy of Princes*, emphasising his right to rule and detailing his ancient royal lineage. It further asked him not to make the same mistakes as his father, urged him to support the crown through his own resources and not Parliament, advised against overspending and excessive generosity and encouraged him to punish those who sought to subvert the peace of the realm. This latter was a veiled reference to the Yorkists and suggests that such people should be dealt with before they could do great harm; it may have equally be read as a criticism of his father's lack of action. Edward was being prepared mentally and academically for reclaiming the throne and restoring the lost glories of the House of Lancaster. Clearly the remaining members of the dynasty and their allies spent much of their time reflecting on what had gone wrong.[1]

Sir Robert Whittingham was present at Koeur with his wife, Catherine, who shared Margaret's Angevin heritage and had been a servant and friend of the queen for more than twenty years. It wasn't unknown for ladies-in-waiting or other attendants who came over with foreign queens or princesses to marry into English gentry in this manner. Katherine Swynford (*née* Roët), originally from Flanders and probably having come over with the retinue of Queen Philippa of Hainault, married an English knight and later the Duke of Lancaster. Another knight, Sir William Vaux, was present at Margaret's court in exile and his wife, Katherine Vaux, was one of Margaret's closest and most loyal attendants, remaining by her side for most of her life. Katherine and William had a son, also called William, who was born around 1460. Another of the refugees was not so lucky: Sir William Grimsby left his wife behind in England and she divorced him during his time in exile. A similar thing happened to Henry Holland, Duke of Exeter, who had been married to Edward IV's sister. He made it to France and eventually found his way to the queen's court.

The Earl of Devon had been executed after the Battle of Towton, but by Christmas 1464 his two younger brothers, John and Henry, had both found a place with Margaret. John styled himself Earl of Devon, although his title was not recognised in England because of what had happened to his brother and because he failed to submit to Edward IV. The Duke of Somerset also came that Christmas, but this was not Henry Beaufort, the duke of old. In May 1464, he had been executed.

Hedgeley Moor and Hexham

Beaufort, as we have seen, had submitted to Edward IV and had reportedly been close the king; they hunted together and were even said to have shared a bedchamber. In December 1463, however, Beaufort remembered his Lancastrian sympathies and fled from his castle of Chirk in Wales to Bamburgh, where he met Henry and was warmly received. He quickly began leading plans for an insurrection against Edward IV.

Edward's first four years on the throne had been troubled to say the least, with constant Lancastrian agitating and sporadic outbreaks of violence akin to the events of the early 1450s. Although he had managed to make treaties with the Scots, French and Burgundians, domestic problems were Edward's biggest issue because so many members of the Lancastrian nobility had escaped and remained at large or were willing to rebel against him at the drop of a hat. Edward was also having trouble with the common people. He was taxing the populace heavily and using the money for defence, although it appeared that armies were often put into the field and then withdrawn. Europe was still also in the grip of a recession, so it was not hard to find disgruntled people who were willing to rebel or rise against the king – especially when it was believed things had been better under Henry. Anti-government disturbances were recorded in Wales and various English counties. These weren't directly caused by Somerset, but his presence and his renewed Lancastrian loyalties were probably the catalyst. Edward quelled most of these disturbances and had some men executed in Chester, once the heartland of the Lancastrian dynasty, and believed that there was no more danger.

Margaret and Henry Beaufort, Duke of Somerset decided to combine their efforts. Over the spring of 1464, he gathered rebels to him in Bamburgh Castle while Margaret worked to gain French support for another invasion of England. Had

Margaret's eagerly awaited troops materialised, the course of the conflict – and indeed English history – may have been very different, but in the event Somerset seems to have opted for guerrilla tactics, preferring to take castles and harry the Yorkists when they were involved in negotiations with the Scots. All he really succeeded in doing was threatening the Yorkist supply base at Newcastle, which forced Edward IV to postpone a Scottish embassy and move its location from Newcastle to York. Edward IV then sent John Neville, Lord Montagu north, ostensibly to escort the Scottish ambassadors safely to York. However, Montagu was a seasoned fighter and military leader and it is not hard to discern that his true purpose was to root out Lancastrian resistance. Somerset decided this would be the perfect opportunity to ambush Montagu and deprive Edward of one of his most important commanders. He nearly succeeded.

One Humphrey Neville, a cousin, was poised to attack with a force of archers and about eighty men-at-arms when Montagu's scouts learned of their presence and warned their commander. He was able to avoid the planned ambush by taking another route and decided to pick up some extra troops at Newcastle to provide him and the ambassadors with more security before heading for Alnwick. On 25 April, while continuing his journey, Montagu found his path blocked by a Lancastrian army under the command of the Duke of Somerset, the indefatigable Lord Hungerford, Ralph Neville and a few others straddling the moorland near Alnwick. The 'battle' of Hedgeley Moor is today considered little more than a skirmish and only involved around 5,000 men. At some point Sir Ralph Neville was killed, destroying Lancastrian morale and causing most of their troops to flee, at which point Montagu was able to go safely on his way.

Montagu was able to escape Hedgeley Moor unscathed and achieve his objective of escorting the Scottish ambassadors to York. For Edward IV, his reappearance was a godsend. He had been preparing to engage the Lancastrians in battle, gathering forces and artillery, and when he heard that Somerset and the other Lancastrians had regrouped forces and were moving to the Tyne Valley he had just the right man for the job on hand. The Lancastrians had learned of Edward's military preparations, and that he was mustering a large army at Leicester. They elected to force a battle. This time, Somerset decided to bring Henry with him, hoping that the presence of the deposed king would shore up wavering Lancastrian morale. When accompanying their forces south, Henry wore a magnificent crown with a double circlet representing his rule over England and France.[2]

On 15 May, the Lancastrian army was encamped a few miles outside Hexham, and Henry was sent to the safety of Byfield Castle. As in previous instances, while the Lancastrian army was happy to bring Henry along for the march, as soon as it seemed like there might be any fighting he was typically deposited nearby to avoid risking his life in combat. He was unlikely to do much good on the battlefield anyway.

Montagu met the Lancastrians the same day, 15 May, and routed them in the vicious Battle of Hexham. His force was actually quite small, numbering only around 4,000 men, but his victory was decisive, sending the Lancastrian commanders fleeing across the countryside. The defeat was not just embarrassing; it was devastating. Somerset was captured shortly after the battle, and three of the other commanders – Lords Hungerford and Moleyns, as well as John, Lord Roos, half-brother of the Earl of Somerset – were found two days later. Edward IV enacted bloody revenge after the Battle of Hexham. He had 'no fewer than thirty' Lancastrians beheaded in the days following the battle, including Somerset in the city of Hexham, and Hungerford and Moleyns at Pontefract.[3] The entirety of the remaining Lancastrian leadership was cut down in the space of a month and King Henry himself was forced to go on the run from Edward's men. They came very close to catching him and even managed to track his movements to Bywell Castle, where he reportedly left his crown and robes behind in his rush to evade his pursuers.

Aside from Henry, about the only Lancastrian commander who escaped the carnage following Hexham was Sir Ralph Grey. He made his way to Bamburgh Castle, along with his friend Sir Humphrey Neville. They made a heroic last stand at the castle in the closing days of June. Yorkist heralds arrived to demand their surrender on the 24th, and when they refused a siege was laid. Leading the besiegers were the Earl of Warwick and his brother, Montagu, who had just been awarded the lands and titles of the Earl of Northumberland. They had been tasked with retaking all the castles that had fallen to the Lancastrians that spring, and Bamburgh was the last. The Lancastrians held out until, under a barrage of artillery fire, the castle was badly damaged and Grey himself was injured. Humphrey Neville eventually submitted and was spared, but Grey was not so fortunate. He was beheaded, and possibly impaled, under the supervision of the notorious Yorkist lord Sir John Tiptoft, later dubbed 'the butcher of England' because of his reported penchant for torture and impalement.

With the final capture of Bamburgh by July 1464, the last bastion of Lancastrian resistance in the north of England crumbled; with the deaths of Somerset and the other military men, Margaret's support network crumbled. Few high-ranking Lancastrian loyalists remained in England, and most of them had joined Margaret at Koeur either on a temporary or permanent basis by the Christmas of 1464. For the first two years of the period in which she resided in France, Margaret maintained regular contact with her husband in England through intermediaries and envoys. Together, they were able to devise plans, schemes and even full-scale invasions. Even in exile, Margaret was a force to be reckoned with and an invaluable asset to her dethroned husband. It is very likely that Christmas was spent formulating plans discussing the future. The following Christmas, that future was even more bleak.

Henry VI Captured

In 1465, Henry VI's luck finally ran out. For nearly a year he had managed to give his Yorkist pursuers the slip, zipping from place to place, always remaining one step ahead. He travelled often as a nondescript and plainly dressed man to make it easier to evade capture. Hostile Yorkist chroniclers suggested that he wandered around like a madman, although one later and more sympathetic source claimed that he was warned in a vision of his capture more than two weeks before. His movements are a mystery, and tall tales have sprung up to fill the gap, but he seems to have been hosted by Lancastrian loyalists and sympathizers. He spent some time in Bolton in Yorkshire where he was hosted by Sir Ralph Pudsey.

On 13 July, he was having dinner at Waddington Hall in Lancashire. There with him was Sir Richard Tunstall, knight, his faithful former chamberlain. Their host was another Richard, Sir Richard Tempest. In the middle of their meal, armed men burst into the great hall; among them was Sir John Tempest, brother of the host. Outside the manor, more armed men lay in wait. They had come to arrest Henry. A ruckus ensued in which Tunstall reportedly drew his sword to fight off those who wanted to capture his king. In the confusion, Henry himself managed to escape from the manor and gallop away on his horse. His adversaries again gave chase, and this time they caught up with him as he was trying to cross the River Ribble a short distance away. It was not just pure good fortune which allowed Henry to be successfully captured on this occasion, however; it is more than likely that he was betrayed. The price on his head was large enough to sway anyone. Given Sir John Tempest's presence, he may even had been betrayed by his host.

Whatever the circumstances, the captive Henry was hastily dispatched to London. He arrived in the capital city on 24 July, marking the first time in more than four years that he had set foot in the capital. Whereas he had been a virtual prisoner of the Earl of Warwick on the previous occasion, this time he was an actual prisoner. It is said that on the day of his arrival he once again met the Earl of Warwick, who formally arrested him, and was then paraded around the city before being committed to the Tower of London.

Henry's capture was of course a major setback for Margaret. It was much harder for her to restore him to the throne when he was locked up in the Tower of London, and it is probable her hopes came to rest more than ever on her son, who was now approaching his twelfth birthday. She still worked tirelessly for the restoration of the House of Lancaster, however. As early as February 1465 she was once more petitioning King Louis of France for support. After Henry's capture, her contacts still kept her up to speed with events in England, and they were beginning to hear rumours of a possible rift between Edward IV and the Earl of Warwick. The cause of the rift is usually put down to Edward's clandestine marriage to the widow Elizabeth Woodville, which took place at some point in 1464. Warwick only found out about the marriage while he was in the middle of negotiating a marriage for Edward with a European princess, causing him great embarrassment.

Margaret set about trying to exploit these divisions at the earliest possible juncture. As early as 1467, she was visited by her older brother, John of Calabria. The siblings had always been close; John had escorted Margaret and her entourage when she left to marry King Henry back in 1445. He had visited her several times in her exile and was even rumoured to have been planning to join one of her invasion attempts. He was thoroughly committed to regaining the

English throne for her husband and her son. Tradition has it that three months before his visit to Margaret in 1467, John of Calabria met with King Louis of France at Bourges. Conversation soon turned to the Earl of Warwick and events in England. King Louis, in what may have been a deliberate attempt to bait his companion, said he preferred Warwick over Henry, which resulted in a heated discussion between the two and Calabria loudly lambasting the king for supporting the English earl over his sister, who was his kin. It is during the record of the same exchange that the following passage appears concerning Prince Edward of Westminster:

> This boy, though only thirteen years of age, already talks of nothing but cutting off heads or making war, as if he had everything in his hands or was the god of battle or the peaceful occupant of [the English] throne.[4]

This statement is now notorious as it is used as evidence that Margaret's son was evil, violent and unsuited to rule. Yet this is a fundamental misunderstanding of the concept of kingship. Edward IV was loved because he looked and acted like a king, and his streak of ruthlessness was probably appreciated by some. The most important thing was that it enabled him to survive. Kings were still expected to be martial and warlike, and the thirteen-year-old Edward was probably just trying to live up to this standard. This is borne out by remarks made by his tutor, Sir John Fortescue, who asserted that he was constantly practising martial skills, and daringly rode 'half tamed' horses while doing so.

He made these observations with the consternation of an educator wishing his student devoted more time and energy to academic exercises like the study of the law, but they help place the Milanese ambassador's remarks in context, and humanise the prince more, distancing him from the caricature sometimes drawn today.[5]

The idea that he spoke as if he was already king may have something to do with the King of France having remarked on how 'arrogantly' Margaret of Anjou came across in her letters to him. In the full context of this exchange, it could have also been a reference to how the prince took after his mother, suggesting he had inherited determination and a strong will from the Angevin side of the family. A preoccupation with battle and warfare would not have been considered unusual for a thirteen-year-old boy in the fifteenth century; perhaps it is simply that Edward had been raised to believe it was his duty to retake his father's throne.[6]

Later in 1467, Edward of Westminster was struck down with a serious bout of illness. His illness put paid to Margaret's plans for handing him over to the King of France as a potential surety for any alliance, and it also meant she did not have to go to Rouen, where King Louis had been intending to meet the Earl of Warwick. The illness in question may have been measles or smallpox. Measles is what we would now consider a childhood disease, but Edward IV himself had been laid low with it for a time, and before vaccination it was a serious disease, sometimes fatal, even for adults. Whatever the nature of Edward's illness, it was clearly serious enough for physicians to be summoned and for Margaret to later go on pilgrimage to give thanks for his recovery.

In 1468, King Louis was sounding out the idea of allying with the Earl of Warwick to restore King Henry to the throne, demonstrating that he was perhaps aware of the tensions between the two men. However, Louis was a cunning political operator, earning the nickname 'the universal spider'. He was more interested in playing different parties off against one another than in taking a side. This was probably the reason why he was inconsistent in his support for the Lancastrians and kept his options open with Warwick and Edward IV. If it benefited him to exploit divisions and destabilise things in England, then he would do that. If it favoured him to encourage a Lancastrian resurgence, he would support it.

Such divisions weren't caused entirely by Edward's secret marriage and the influence of his queen's Woodville relatives but also by Warwick's resentment at his loss of power. For the first few years of his reign, Edward IV was quite content to leave most things to the Nevilles and they soon became the power behind the throne. In June 1469, however, Warwick and his allies instigated a large-scale rebellion in the north, which was in truth the cover for a Neville coup. By the time Edward figured out the trap, his forces had been overcome at the Battle of Edgcote and he had been captured. The King of England was now a prisoner of the Earl of Warwick. Perhaps he understood how Henry VI felt in 1461. Warwick then tried to exert his authority through Edward in a similar way as he had with the Lancastrian king, but simply putting Edward IV on display and producing him whenever he wanted to invoke royal authority did not work; Edward was not content to remain a captive puppet. Compounding his troubles, Warwick had opened a can of worms in the north, and the men of the region suddenly remembered their long dormant Lancastrian sympathies. Within a few weeks of the Battle of Edgcote, another rebellion. This time, it was conducted in the name of King Henry and its leader was Humphrey Neville – he who had been a leader of the 1464 campaign which had culminated in the Battle of Hexham. To gain the military support he needed to put down this rebellion, Warwick was forced to release the captive Edward IV.

Although Edward officially forgave Warwick, their relationship was fraught. The situation was made even more delicate by the fact that Edward's younger brother George, Duke of Clarence was firmly in Warwick's camp and had married his daughter Isabel. The following year, Warwick tried once again to seize power. A rebellion began in Lincolnshire, this time spearheaded by Lord Richard Welles and his son Robert. Some of their retainers were wearing Warwick's livery, indicating that the earl may well have instigated the rebellion. His plan, apparently, was to trap King Edward when he went to deal with the rebels in Lincolnshire by coming from Yorkshire with his own forces. This failed when Edward stamped out the rebellion and had Robert Welles executed despite having promised him a pardon. Deprived of support, and now engaged in open rebellion against the king, Warwick had no choice but to flee along with his son-in-law the Duke of Clarence, his wife and his daughter. They sailed across the Channel but, ironically, were denied entry to Calais, which was still English and therefore Edward's territory.

Instead, the family landed at Honfleur on 1 May 1470. The wheel of fortune had turned, and now Margaret of Anjou's deadliest enemy was on French soil, having become like her a fugitive and an avowed enemy of the King of England. Margaret was understandably wary. Her surviving correspondence, rare for this period, includes a letter warning merchants in Lubeck against dealing with either Edward IV or the Earl of Warwick. These merchants were part of what would become known as the Hanseatic League, a powerful and wealthy mercantile corporation whose support was vital to anyone seeking ships or the money to launch them.[7] The letter was written in Latin instead of her usual French, demonstrating her multilingual skills.

More than a month passed before Margaret was convinced to come to terms with Warwick, and it took even longer for her to leave her refuge at Koeur to attend negotiations. She arrived on 23 June 1470 in the town of Amboise in the Loire Valley, where Louis and the earl were waiting for her. She was warmly received, but negotiations proceeded at a painfully slow pace. On 28 June, the Milanese ambassador, watching the proceedings, reported:

> His majesty has spent and still spends every day in long discussions with that queen to induce her to make the alliance with Warwick and to let the prince, her son, go with the earl to the enterprise of England. Up to the present the queen has shown herself very hard and difficult, and although his majesty offers her many assurances, it seems

that on no account whatever will she agree to send her son with Warwick, as she mistrusts him.[8]

Women, of course, were not supposed to be 'hard and difficult', but Margaret had every reason to be. Warwick seemed to expect Margaret to simply pardon him and forgive everything he had done over the last two decades. But he had not just harmed her. He had done great injury to her friends and allies, some of whom resided with her, among them Edmund Beaufort, younger brother of the Duke of Somerset. There was much arguing back and forth over the next month, and at some point the matter of marrying Edward to the young Anne Neville was probably raised. On 22 July, at Angers Cathedral, Margaret finally met Warwick in person for the first time in more than a decade. She humiliated him by making him stay on his knees for more than fifteen minutes while she admonished him.

Three days later, the sixteen-year-old Edward of Westminster was formally betrothed to Anne Neville, the fourteen-year-old daughter of the Earl of Warwick, in Angers Cathedral. On the same day, Warwick formally swore himself to the cause of Lancaster, and Margaret swore to accept Warwick as her liegeman. A few days later, Warwick set sail for England with Clarence, Jasper Tudor and John de Vere, Earl of Oxford. They were on their way to fulfil their part of the bargain by ousting Edward IV and restoring Henry VI to the throne of England. Prince Edward did not come with them; Margaret refused to allow him to return to England until his father was secure on the throne. She could only hope and pray that their plan would succeed.

9

VICTORY AND DEATH

In less than two months, Warwick and his allies would succeed in their mission. They arrived back in England on 13 September 1470. Lancastrian supporters quickly flocked to them, although they were probably inspired to do so by the presence of de Vere and Tudor, not Warwick. By October, Edward IV had fled along with his youngest brother Richard. He had been taken entirely by surprise, having been in Yorkshire fending off yet another uprising at the time of the Lancastrian landing, and when he tried to move south he found that Montagu had defected to his brother's cause. Having no friends or supporters left, and with his life in imminent danger, Edward limped to the Netherlands.

On either 3 or 6 October, after five years of captivity, Henry VI was released from his quarters in the Tower of London. He was greeted by William Waynflete, once his friend, and by the mayor and aldermen of London. They came to tell Henry that he was once again king, and then escorted him to Westminster. Sadly, Henry did not cut an impressive figure. Shabbily clothed, he was not arrayed like a king. Waynflete had to fetch more suitable clothes for him before they took him to Westminster and returned to him the regalia and robes of kingship. Thus began his second reign, known as the Readeption.

A few days later, Warwick and Clarence met with the king. Kneeling, they swore fealty to him. On 13 October, which might also have been Edward of Westminster's seventeenth birthday, Warwick decided that Henry should go on a grand procession through London and make himself known to the people. Parliament was then summoned for a meeting in November. This session was dated to the forty-ninth year of the reign of King Henry VI, effectively erasing Edward IV's reign from the records. Very little happened in this parliament, the first and only one of Henry's second reign. Edward IV and his brother Richard of Gloucester were attainted, but everyone who accepted Henry was allowed to keep their place. Elizabeth Woodville, who had claimed sanctuary in Westminster Abbey, was allowed to stay there in peace. The only execution was that of the deeply unpopular John Tiptoft, Earl of Worcester. It may have been John de Vere who pushed for this, as revenge for Tiptoft having presided over the execution of his father and brother back in 1462.

Although people flocked to the capital to see Henry, his emotional and mental condition would probably have been fragile. After five years of confinement, he naturally didn't look very regal. Contrary to popular belief today, noble prisoners were not kept in dungeons at this time and were in fact usually lodged in some comfort, but it is said that Henry didn't change his clothes very often and mostly wore an old blue gown. Naturally, he probably became more introverted and pious in his years of captivity. It may actually have been a relief to him to be freed from the burden of kingship, which never seemed to suit him too well, though he never wanted to lose his crown.

Although Henry was now back on the throne, the wounds of the last decade were not healed. There were holes in the Readeption regime from the beginning. At the November parliament, the Acts of Attainder passed against Lancastrian lords were reversed, but it was not as simple as just returning lands to their previous holders. Many of their estates had been given away and divided up among others, and Warwick's supporters in particular had much to lose from any redistribution of land. The Duke of Clarence also had no loyalty to Henry, being motivated by animosity to his brother Edward and a desire to please his father-in-law Warwick. However, Warwick was changeable and had switched sides at the drop of a hat before. Perhaps the biggest problem of the regime was that it didn't change anything. This had been an issue for the previous regime too. Edward IV had failed to deliver on his father's promised programme of reform despite his decade in charge, and his reign had been plagued by near constant discontent and rebellion. He seemed to be little more than a younger, more handsome and less pious Henry VI, who came without the forceful and controversial wife (although his marriage proved controversial in its own ways). All the new regime did was promise peace.

Meanwhile, in France, Margaret and her son were kicking their heels. There was one major snag in the alliance they had made with Louis of France, and it was that he required Warwick and his allies to attack the Duke of Burgundy as soon as they were able to do so. He would not let Margaret return to England until this was done. With her were her son and the young Anne Neville, who were finally married in December 1470. Recent historians have suggested that Margaret mistreated Anne because of the animosity she had towards her father, but there is no evidence for this. It is more likely that Margaret felt some sympathy for Anne, who was then barely fifteen years old, the same age as she herself had been when she married King Henry.

It is also commonly claimed that Anne and Prince Edward's marriage was never consummated because Margaret treated it only as a temporary settlement and eventually hoped for a better match. While this is possible, and Margaret had indeed been resistant to the marriage, it is more likely that it was consummated – especially since Louis had gone to great lengths to secure papal dispensations for the two young people to marry. Margaret, in making the alliance with Warwick, had put herself entirely at the mercy of the King of France and she did not dare to defy or upset him.

As the year of 1470 came to an end, King Louis was losing patience. He was pressing Warwick on the matter of going to war with Burgundy. In January 1471, he decided to make the first move and commence war against Burgundy, expecting Warwick to join him. On 17 February 1471, Warwick wrote to King Louis confirming that he would soon do so. Strangely, it was the King of France's attack upon the Duke of Burgundy and Warwick's agreement to join him that turned the tide of events in England. Charles, Duke of Burgundy had been reluctant to align with or support the exiled Edward IV, who had been residing in his lands, but as 1471 dawned, with Louis threatening his borders and the Earl of Warwick threatening to invade by sea, the Duke of Burgundy decided to meet Edward IV. He was officially a supporter of the Lancastrians and had a treaty with England, but he was married to Margaret of York, none other than Edward IV's sister, and she wanted to help her family.

Despite this, Charles's support for York had been inconsistent. In the years before he had provided the Duke of Somerset with an annuity and Somerset had fought alongside him in a military campaign. He considered Somerset to be a friend, and so supporting the deposed Yorkist king was not a decision he made lightly. Indeed, it was only due to his wife's influence that Edward had a haven in Burgundian lands over the winter of 1470, and it may have been at her instigation that the two men met to discuss an alliance. Although officially he did not give Edward any aid because of the treaty, he secretly gifted Edward's campaign a vast sum of money and a few ships. It was in Charles's interests to prevent the invasion of his territory, even if that meant helping Edward get back to England to reclaim the throne.

In the closing days of February, a truly remarkable situation ensued in which both Edward IV and Margaret of Anjou, alongside their retainers, headed for ports to secure passage across the English Channel. It was a race, although Margaret probably was not aware of it; the port Edward chose was Vlissingen in the modern-day Netherlands, she headed for Honfleur in Normandy. Departing from Vlissingen, called Flushing by the English, Edward arrived in early March with some 1,200 troops. He had spent the Duke of Burgundy's money wisely and hired Flemish and English mercenaries. Both he and Margaret were hampered by storms in the Channel, and their vessels were forced to remain in their respective ports while in England both Henry and the Earl of Warwick waited with bated breath for news. Edward IV won the race and managed to set sail on 11 March. We do not know when he landed, but according to tradition it may have been as early as 14 March. Early reports said that he tried to make landfall in Norfolk but was driven back and prevented from disembarking by the Earl of Oxford, and then continued bad weather and storms drove his ships north. Eventually, he was able to disembark at Ravenspur in Yorkshire. This was the same place where, seventy-two years earlier, Henry Bolingbroke had arrived in England from his own exile, claiming that he only wished to reclaim his estates and titles as the Duke of Lancaster, shortly before deposing King Richard II and claiming the throne himself as Henry IV.

Edward IV tried the same trick. He was able to move unmolested through Yorkshire with his army because of reassurances that he had not returned to make war on the king but simply to reclaim his birthright as the Duke of York. It was on this basis that he was allowed to enter the city of York, where it is claimed he 'led a chorus of cheers for King Henry' and made solemn oaths that he had not come to steal the crown.[1]

By then, Henry and Warwick had heard of Edward's activities and were taking evasive action. Warwick was dispatched to Coventry where he raised a large army, and Henry remained in London with Edmund Beaufort, Duke of Somerset, who had returned from long years of exile in France. While they waited, Edward made steady progress. By the time he got to Doncaster, he had dropped all pretence and made clear his intention to reclaim the crown. Montagu, Warwick's brother, allowed him to march through his own lands unopposed, as did many other lords. It is an open question as to why they did not stand against Edward. Some historians insist that it was because all the English nobility were still loyal to the House of York, but it is just as probable they were hedging their bets. Most would have realised that a battle was inevitable and did not want to be on the losing side.

Another who sat still was Henry Percy, Earl of Northumberland, who had been restored to his lands by Henry the previous year. Once Edward reached the Midlands, troops under the command of his long-time supporter and friend William, Lord Hastings flocked to him.

While all of this was going on, Warwick waited in Coventry. He refused to do battle with the Yorkists, claiming he was waiting for the Duke of Clarence to arrive. On 3 April, he finally received news that Clarence had arrived with his men at Banbury in Oxfordshire, but the details proved this wasn't the good news he wanted to hear. Clarence's men were wearing a symbol of the white rose; he had switched sides and was going to join his brother. This defection was not sudden or spontaneous. Clarence and Edward's mother, Cecily Neville, and his sister Margaret of York had been working on him, reminding him that he had nothing to gain from the Lancastrians and urging him to remember his loyalty to his family. It worked, and Clarence intentionally bypassed Warwick's forces to join his older brother. Together they marched for London.

On 10 April, the capital received two letters: one from the Earl of Warwick and the other from Edward. Each warned of imminent attack and instructed the people of the city to arrange their own defence. Henry was taken from his lodgings and paraded through the streets in an attempt to rally people to Warwick's cause, but the reality was that George Neville had already written to Edward to appeal for mercy and save his own skin. Henry's final procession through the city failed to impress the common people, and when Edward arrived outside the capital a few days later the gates were thrown open for him.

The unfortunate Henry, who had been restored to his throne for less than six months, was Edward's prisoner once again. It is said that when Edward returned to London he was escorted to the Tower, where the naive Henry greeted the man who had deposed him warmly, saying, 'Cousin of York, you are very welcome. I know my life will be safe in your hands.'[2]

Edward decided to take Henry with him to face Warwick's army. So it was that on the morning of 14 April 1471, which also happened to be Easter Day, Henry found himself sitting and watching from Edward IV's camp as his usurper prepared to do battle with the man who had helped to put that usurper on his throne in the first place. The site was near Chipping Barnet, which was then a small town outside of London. Uncle prepared to fight nephew over the crown of England on a plain of grass and heathland called Enfield Chase about a mile from the town. A thick mist hung in the air that day, rendering visibility poor and preventing the troops from being able to make out their opponents until they drew lethally close. Indeed, it is said that as the two armies fought it out nobody could tell who was winning or losing, and the men did not know if they were even fighting those on their own side.

The decisive moment in the battle was a result of the actions of the Lancastrian loyalist John de Vere, Earl of Oxford. He charged and attacked the Yorkist's left flank, which was under the command of Lord Hastings. The Yorkist flank quickly broke and ran, with the Lancastrians giving chase. So far so good, but then discipline broke down among Oxford's troops. Distracted from the battle, some fell to looting despite Oxford's attempts to establish order. Meanwhile, the centre ranks of the opposing armies were led by Edward and Warwick. The two seem to have been evenly matched, but Edward's right flank, led by his younger brother Richard, Duke of Gloucester, inflicted severe damage on the Lancastrian left flank under the command of the Duke of Exeter.

In the thick fog, the main body of the Yorkist army didn't even notice the total collapse of its left flank. Some of Hastings' troops even ran all the way back to London and proclaimed that the Lancastrians had won. After managing to regroup, however, Hastings marched them back to the field to engage with the enemy once more.

What happened next is uncertain, but it appears that the armies, amid the chaos of fighting and fog, had shifted positions – that, or Oxford simply became lost, because he came upon a division of Montagu's Lancastrian soldiers and did not recognise them as his comrades. In turn, when Montagu's troops saw the approaching men, Oxford's banner of a white five-pointed star was mistaken for Edward's emblem of the sun in splendour (a white rose surrounded by sunbeams) and they attacked. Cries of 'treason!' went up from Oxford's men as they realised they had been attacked by their own side, thinking it the result of betrayal rather than confusion. As a result, discipline among the Lancastrian troops entirely broke down and the army abandoned the field. In the chaos, both Montagu and Warwick himself were killed, reportedly while trying to escape on foot into nearby woodland. The day was won by the House of York, and Edward marched in triumph back to London, where he consigned King Henry to the

Tower yet again. This time, George Neville was sent to join him.

In a final savage twist of fortune, 14 April was the same day that Margaret of Anjou and her son Prince Edward finally arrived back in England. For weeks they had been attempting to cross the Channel but had been foiled by the poor weather conditions. Margaret set foot on English soil for the first time in seven years as she disembarked at Weymouth. The following day, when staying at Cerne Abbey, she received news of the Battle of Barnet and its outcome. Henry was back in the Tower, and the bodies of Warwick and Montagu had been put on public display to prove that they were dead.

At first Margaret panicked; she wanted to get back on her ship and immediately return to France with her son, but her commanders, the Duke of Somerset and the John Courtenay, encouraged her to stay and fight. They suggested that the death of the Earl of Warwick could actually work in their favour, reasoning that the man's loyalty had never been assured whereas now she only had to work with people whose loyalty was beyond dispute.

The two men themselves raised what troops they could on the course of their march through the West Country, but this must have been a challenge as they had only returned to England and seen their lands restored in February, barely two months earlier. Their intention was to reach Wales, where Margaret planned to join forces with her long-time ally Jasper Tudor, and then to hasten to the Lancastrian heartlands in Chester and the north where they planned to muster more troops and artillery. The problem was that the Lancastrian commanders were scattered, as were all their potential troops. They also tried to make the enemy believe that they were heading for London. By 24 April, Edward IV had received word of the Lancastrians' arrival, mustered his own troops and set out to meet them. In the opening days of May there ensued a dramatic chase, with Edward's army closing in on the Lancastrians. One night, the Lancastrians passed within 4 miles of Edward's position in a desperate bid to reach Wales before the Yorkist host intercepted them.

By 2 May, Edward was at Malmesbury. Here he was told that the Lancastrian force had passed through Bristol and found a haven at Berkeley. Yet when the Lancastrians got to Gloucester on 3 May, the gates were shut against them thanks to Edward sending word ahead to one of his servants, Sir Richard Beauchamp. The Lancastrians still had to cross the River Severn, and since Gloucester was barred to them they had apparently decided to head for the next major bridge at Upton upon Severn. The exhausted Lancastrians, who had been marching for days trying to stay ahead of their enemies, were finally intercepted just outside Tewkesbury on 3 May. By that time, Margaret could go no further. She was with Anne Neville and Katherine Vaux, and the three women, like their troops, were exhausted. They probably retired to the nearby Glupshill Manor, and they would have known that battle was inevitable.

The Lancastrians opted to deploy their troops on a good strategic position on slightly sloped grazing land dotted with ditches and hedges. Even at this point, however, there was division among the Lancastrian leadership. Somerset believed that they should stand and fight, but Lord Wenlock favoured retreating to Wales and not engaging the enemy until they had joined with Tudor. It is easy, with hindsight, to see Wenlock as the wise and level-headed one, but he was also a notorious and serial turncoat. He had once been a servant of Henry VI but changed to the Yorkist side in the late 1450s and may have been acting as a double agent during negotiations with France. He had then sided with Warwick against Edward IV and was now fighting for Lancaster against Edward. He was not trusted, and he was proposing a course of action that seemed unrealistic.

The following day, 4 May, Edward IV donned his armour and the two armies formed ranks. Although the Lancastrian force was larger, Edward had the advantage that his men were not exhausted by a long forced march across rough terrain. They were also better equipped, and Edward had been able to obtain fresh troops on his way from London without relying on mercenaries. What they lacked in numbers they therefore made up for in energy, and they also had better artillery, including some which they had captured from the Lancastrians. Prince Edward was placed in the central division of the Lancastrian army, although he did not actually command it; that task fell to the shifty Lord Wenlock. Somerset's plan had been formulated, and his decision was that Wenlock and the prince's forces should attack from the front while he launched a surprise attack from the side. However, Richard of Gloucester made an unexpected assault up the hill. For an hour and more,

Yorkist archers subjected their enemies to deadly barrages of arrows. Somerset's division meanwhile bore the brunt of the artillery fire, which inflicted many casualties.

It is at this point that things become unclear. One version of events says that Richard of Gloucester sounded a false retreat and Somerset gave chase, breaking ranks to lead his men on a headlong charge down the hill.[3] Another version says that Somerset tried to make a feint and outflank Edward's men, having spotted that he would be able to swing some of his troops around, and 'succeeded in bringing his troops to a sloping field from which they were able to launch a downhill attack on the flank' of Edward's forces.[4] His strategy very nearly worked, but the problem was that it took the pressure off the centre of Edward's forces and allowed Richard of Gloucester, who commanded the vanguard, to come to his brother's aid. Somerset was beaten back. As he was forced to retreat up the slope, his forces found themselves between Edward's main army and a group of 200 spearmen strategically positioned in woodland – although another version says that these 200 spearmen engaged Somerset's men during the main battle, and not as they were retreating.[5]

Somerset's men fought valiantly, but they were surrounded and slaughtered. When the opportunity arose the remainder broke and ran, and during the rout many were cut down while others reportedly drowned.

A few survivors were gathered and with their commander limped back towards the main Lancastrian army. When Somerset arrived he was furious, and not without cause. He had shouted for Lord Wenlock to join him and charge at the Yorkists together with the prince and all their forces. Such a combined charge *could* have been successful: if the entire Lancastrian army had smashed into the Yorkists' centre they could well have beaten them back. Instead, Wenlock had intentionally held back and had ordered the prince to do the same. He had simply stood by, watching while Somerset's men engaged the enemy alone and faced slaughter. There was no apparent tactical justification for Wenlock's inaction, so Somerset accused him of being a traitor before attacking him with an axe, splitting his head open and killing him instantly.

Meanwhile, the Yorkists had regrouped and launched an attack on the central part of the Lancastrian army. The seventeen-year-old Prince Edward was now left to command them alone, and although he attempted to keep order among his men the attack was too strong and too vicious. Chaos ensued. The main body of the Lancastrian army either did not know what had happened to Somerset's vanguard or heard they had been massacred, and then the commanders fell to fighting one another. There were shouts of treason, and with Edward's renewed attack the Lancastrian lines collapsed. As the battle was lost, men fled in all directions, some towards the River Avon and others into the parks and meadows. Now the Yorkists gave chase, and nearly 2,000 men died in the battle and the rout. Many fled towards Tewkesbury Abbey, and it was there that so many were cut down that the site was thereafter known as 'the bloody meadow'. At the end of the day, the slain included the Earl of Devon and Somerset's younger brother John Beaufort as well as Sir Nicholas Vaux, the husband of Margaret's lady-in-waiting.

Accounts of what happened next differ considerably. The few survivors who managed to get to Tewkesbury Abbey tried to claim sanctuary there. *The Arrivall of Edward IV*, written by an anonymous observer who claimed to have been a servant of Edward IV, said that Edward went into the abbey and gave thanks to God for his victory before magnanimously pardoning everyone involved. Warkworth's Chronicle, however, suggests that the victorious Yorkists chased down their enemies and Edward 'came with his sword into the church' where he had to be stopped by a priest. Other acts of post-battle violence are suggested as well.[6] Some of Edward's men may have begun cutting down Lancastrian soldiers in the abbey itself, and the monks and priests perhaps had to intervene to stop them; we know that shortly afterwards the abbey and its grounds had to be reconsecrated because of all the blood which had been spilled there.

The chief mystery concerns the death of Prince Edward. Most historians say that he died during the rout or the battle itself. One possibility is that he was surrounded or that a squad of troops was sent with the express intention of dispatching him. The Croyland Chronicle, written about fifteen years after the battle, says, 'And there was slain in the field Prince Edward, who cried for succour to his brother-in-law the Duke of Clarence.' However, there is another, darker suggestion. The Great Chronicle of London, composed in the early sixteenth century, asserted that Prince Edward was

> ...brought into his [the King's] presence, after the king had questioned a few words of the cause of his so landing within his realm, and he gave unto the king an answer contrary to his pleasure, the king struck him on the face with the back of his gauntlet, after which stroke so received by him, the king's servants rid him out of life forthwith.[7]

The same story was repeated by Polydore Vergil around 1502 as well as appearing in other, slightly later sources. There was one French source, written within two years of Tewkesbury, which supports the claim that Edward was murdered shortly after the battle, and one very obscure English register claims he was executed after a military tribunal, but aside from these, most of the English sources give an account of him falling during or just before the battle, and the part about his being brought before the king seems to have been a tradition which developed a few years later. It is possible that if such a thing did occur Edward IV would not have wanted it to become public knowledge for the damage it would have done to his reputation. Prince Edward might have died during the battle, but his death could not have been more convenient for the Yorkist king.

Whatever happened, the Battle of Tewkesbury was the end. To all intents and purposes it marked the death of the House of Lancaster and the Lancastrian cause.

Although the Duke of Somerset and several other prominent nobles survived the battle, they were not spared nor pardoned as Edward IV had promised. The Battle of Tewkesbury had taken place on a Saturday, and they went unmolested the following day, but on Monday 6 May all of the leading Lancastrians were taken out of the abbey and subjected to what was essentially a show trial. Inevitably, they were found guilty of treason against Edward IV and executed that day. As many as nineteen men were executed, the most prominent being Edmund Beaufort, Duke of Somerset, the earl of Devon's cousin Hugh Courtenay and, rather shockingly, John Langstrother, the prior of the Order of the Knights Hospitaller in England. He is the man shown in an illustration in *The Arrivall of Edward IV* wearing black robes emblazoned with a white cross as befitting his order. His status as a cleric did not save him from Edward's vengeance.

Most of the nobles who had fallen at Tewkesbury were buried within the abbey, with Prince Edward interred beneath the floor of the choir. Today a Victorian plaque marks his final resting place, although there may have been a memorial brass there originally, and Susan Higginbotham suggests that the tomb may have originally been marked by an elaborate roofed structure known as a 'hearse'. Although the king may have paid for Masses to be said for the young man's soul, it is unlikely that he would have sanctioned an elaborate tomb which might prove an inspirational rallying point for future rebels.

With the deaths of Somerset and Prince Edward, all the surviving Lancastrian claimants in the direct male line were dead. The last hopes of the House of Lancaster were snuffed out at the point of the sword and the edge of an axe. Margaret and her newly widowed daughter-in-law Anne Neville were found a few days later in a religious house where they had taken refuge with Margaret's faithful lady-in-waiting Katherine Vaux, yet another widow of the battle.

Margaret offered no resistance when she was captured, reportedly by William Stanley. Her worst fears had been realised. Her spirit was finally broken and there was no fight left in her. On 11 May she met with Edward IV at Coventry, an occasion which must have been tense and difficult, although not as dramatic as some later writers would depict it, with her muttering curses and shouting maledictions like a stereotypical distraught woman.[8] Afterwards, the queen was conveyed back to London in a wagon. According to one tradition, she was staring blankly ahead of her and saying nothing for much of the journey. For a time there was talk of having Queen Margaret executed, but this did not happen. She was no longer a threat to the Yorkists, not on her own and with her only child dead. Despite everything, Edward did retain some sense of honour and chivalry, perhaps repaying Henry's courtesy in leaving Edward's pregnant wife in peace when she claimed sanctuary in Westminster Abbey. Margaret was conveyed to the Tower but kept away from her husband. Henry himself died mysteriously in the Tower on 23 May. The Yorkists said he died of 'pure melancholy', but he was almost certainly murdered. Now that his son was dead he could be dispatched without Lancastrian loyalties transferring to someone else.

10

ONCE CALLED QUEEN

After the events of May 1471, Margaret was finally defeated. Everything that she had lived for, everything she valued, everything she had fought for over the space of a decade, and the very purpose for which she was raised, had been torn away from her in one terrible day. Despite her involvement in wars, rebellions and political wrangling, Margaret was always fundamentally the wife of a king and the mother, she had always believed, of a future king. Everything within her had railed against risking the life of her only son to the uncertainty of the battlefield, but she had allowed it. She surely knew that if Prince Edward was ever to be a great king, he had to lead his men. He had to fight for his crown. Instead, at just seventeen years of age, Edward of Westminster had died for it.

It was truly her son who had been the important one. Henry had only been kept alive for six years in the Tower of London because killing him would have shifted the allegiance of the remaining Lancastrians entirely to his son, and Edward was more of a threat then Henry had been for years. This fact almost serves to prove that the Yorkists accepted that Henry VI was Edward's biological father, despite what their propaganda espoused. Yet it was not just Margaret's son who died. She also lost close friends and supporters that day. There was her good friend Edmund Beaufort, the namesake son of the man who had welcomed her to England so many years before and the brother of Henry Beaufort, who had fought so fiercely for the Lancastrian throne. Katherine Vaux had also been widowed at Tewkesbury, something which seems to have only served to draw the two women closer. They were united in grief and loss; Katherine did not blame Margaret for what happened to her or her family.

Mainland Europe soon heard about what had happened in England, and nobody truly believed the story about Henry dying of melancholy. The continent was shocked at what had taken place. In June 1471, a Milanese correspondent wrote thus:

King Edward has not chosen to have the custody of King Henry any longer, although he was in some sense innocent, and there was no great fear about his proceedings, the prince his son and the Earl of Warwick being dead as well as all those who were for him and had any vigour, as he has caused King Henry to be secretly assassinated in the Tower, where he was a prisoner. They say he has done the same to the queen [sic], King Henry's wife. He has, in short, chosen to crush the seed.[1]

Although his sources were obviously incorrect, and he believed that Queen Margaret herself had been put to death, the correspondent nevertheless understood what Edward had done and why. In some parts of Europe, it is possible that Margaret would have been so dispatched. Instead, now that the tiger was toothless, the Yorkists decided to set her at liberty. She was moved out of the Tower and taken at some point to Windsor.

By July she had been moved from there to Wallingford, where she was lodged with one of her oldest friends, Alice Chaucer, Duchess of Suffolk. Alice was of course the widow of the duke who had been murdered two decades before on a boat in the Channel in 1450. Her son, named John, went on to marry one of Edward IV's many sisters. It was through John de la Pole that the once staunchly Lancastrian family went on to become a Yorkist institution, and John's children and grandchildren would be the heirs of the Yorkist dynasty. Alice had a residence at Ewelme, where she was later buried in an impressive cadaver tomb, and was also the custodian of Wallingford Castle.

It was at Wallingford that Margaret seems to have lived for the next few years, although she may well have visited Ewelme as well, finding it a peaceful retreat in the Oxfordshire countryside. Here she could mourn her losses and find perhaps some solace among her friends – Katherine Vaux remained with her.

There is an image from a guild book of the London Skinners' Company in 1475 which depicts Margaret kneeling in prayer with a female attendant, believed to be Katherine Vaux, kneeling behind her. Skinners of course would have provided the fur linings and clothing trims so fashionable for both sexes, and Margaret appears to have joined the guild at some point. It was entirely possible for people who were not members of a profession to join such a group; Queen Elizabeth Woodville was another member. Amy Licence has suggested that one benefit of membership was that the ladies in question were provided with free clothing.[2]

In the illustration, both women wear dark colours. Katherine's dress appears to be dark blue, and Margaret is dressed like a nun complete with what looks like some kind of wimple under her raised hood. The colours that Katherine wore might be associated with mourning since dark blue, not black, was the traditional colour associated with mourning at this time, although she also sports an elaborate headdress as well as fur trim on the bodice of her gown. The two women are reading from what appear to be breviaries, or books of devotion. A crown and sceptre lie discarded on a table nearby, indicating the trappings of queenship set aside. Instead, the image gives the impression that she was pursuing a quiet life coloured by religious devotion. Really, she had no choice. Her image in the guild book also suggests that she spent some time in London in the early 1470s and may even have moved there for a time. Again, this is interesting as her relationship with the capital during her time as queen was problematic to say the least.

In 1475, Alice Chaucer died. Margaret may have attended her funeral when she was laid to rest at St Mary's Church in Ewelme. The same year, Edward IV went to war with France. With the years of war in England a thing of the past and the threats to his rule removed, he decided to take up the traditional occupation of medieval English kings. Unlike the wars in England, however, his campaign in France was an unmitigated disaster. Little was achieved, and no territory was regained. The whole debacle ended in a treaty between Edward IV and Louis XI, and as part of that agreement, which became known as the Treaty of Picquigny, the King of England agreed to 'ransom' Margaret to her cousin for a sum of £50,000. It was an ignominious and ironic conclusion to Margaret's story. For years people had been saying that King Henry 'bought' her from her late uncle at the cost of Maine and England's honour, and she ended up being sold back to France after a failed military expedition, owing to the poverty of the English king who had slain her husband and son.

Even this agreement came with a sting in the tail: in exchange for being allowed to return to her family and receive a pension from the French king, Margaret was forced to renounce her claim to all lands and titles in both England and France. Her Angevin family's holdings were vast, and they were so important to the family that Margaret had incorporated the arms of Anjou and Lorraine into her personal livery. If her son had lived, he or even Margaret herself may well have been able to lay claim to some of them. Her brother John of Calabria, the only surviving son of René, had also been Duke of Lorraine when he died in December 1470. John's son did succeed him as Duke of Lorraine, but he died in 1473 at the age of only twenty-two.

Despite these terms, after Alice Chaucer's death Margaret really had nothing to keep her in England. She was forty-five years old and desperately wanted to return to the land of her birth and the only family which she had left. So, she agreed to Louis's conditions, and in November 1475 she was entrusted into the care of a knight called Sir Thomas Montgomery, who was tasked with escorting her back to France. She was there by the end of the year, and soon went to live with her father at his castle in Reculée, Angers, where she was supposed to be provided with an income of 6,000 crowns a year from the King of France. In truth this was paid 'only intermittently' and was small consolation for having had to sign away all claims to her inheritance.[3] It seems she relied on her father's support.

Margaret lived out the remainder of the 1470s at Reculée, perhaps spending some time hunting in the nearby countryside. We know she owned a pack of hunting dogs, perhaps greyhounds, which would have accompanied her on such expeditions. Her only link to her former life was the faithful Katherine Vaux, who went with her as she had during her period living in exile in the 1460s. Then her father died on 10 July 1480, and once again Margaret was at a loose end. She was unable to live in her father's castle any more as she was not his heir or successor, and her pension was not paid consistently, and so she found herself living off the charity of others. René did try to provide for his widowed daughter, whose life had been plagued by tragedy. In his will, he left her one thousand crowns in cash, as well as an annuity of two thousand livres and one of his castles. Yet at the time of his death, it seems that he was no longer able to pass her either the castle or the annuity. Instead, he entrusted her to the care of his friend Francis de Vignolles, who took her to the castle of Dampierre near Saumur.

Margaret was once again at the mercy of others, and when she moved into what was to be her final home she took solace 'in her literary pursuits and her relics'.[4] This involved reading the works of the Burgundian poet Georges Chastellain, who died in 1475. He wrote everything from a satirical take on court life to a celebration of the French defeating the English. One of his works, the *Temple de Boccace*, in which the moral philosopher Giovanni Boccaccio mused upon the vicissitudes of fortune, was dedicated to her. It was a short treatise that had been intended to bring her some comfort during the time of her exile. She had quite probably known Chastellain personally, as he had been a secretary of her friend Pierre de Brézé and dedicated another of his works to the man. Although *Temple de Boccace* was probably written before Tewkesbury, in the years afterwards she may still have been able to draw comfort from knowing that one of her friends took the trouble to write a book specifically for her.[5]

Margaret lived at Dampierre for two years before falling ill in the summer of 1482. One later source would say that she contracted leprosy, but that is highly unlikely, and medieval medical understanding was so limited that various conditions could have been labelled as such. It is possible that the idea Margaret had leprosy was based on some of the rumours that had gained so much currency in England during her reign and her exile, as leprosy was sometimes interpreted as punishment for immoral and sinful behaviour, and someone claiming she had the disease was probably implying that God was punishing her for her immoral lifestyle in her younger days. There is no evidence and no other corroboration that she had the condition, or anything like it, and as little evidence that Margaret was ever immoral in the way her enemies suggested.

Margaret was fifty-two years old, and although her father had lived to be eighty, it became obvious as the summer of 1482 waned that her death was approaching. If her son had lived, he would have been twenty-eight years old by that time and would probably have made her a grandmother several times over. All of that had been ripped away in a meadow near Tewkesbury Abbey eleven years earlier.

On 2 August, Margaret made her will. She appointed the King of France as her heir, with her only real request being that she was buried with her parents in the church of St Maurice in Angers. She did not have enough money for a funeral, so she requested that the King of France sell her remaining possessions to pay for it. Louis took this very literally, and even before she died he demanded that a friend of Margaret's hand over some valuable hunting dogs she had gifted to him. She died just over three weeks later, on 25 August, with Katherine Vaux and some of her attendants by her side.

Epilogue

MARGARET, MORE SINNED AGAINST THAN SINNER

Only eight months after Margaret's death, her deadliest rival, Edward IV, followed her into the next world. He died in April 1483 at the age of forty-two. The cause of his death is unclear, although one proposed cause was food poisoning. In an era before antibiotics, such a thing could indeed kill even a man like Edward.

The events of the next two years are well known and have been much debated. Edward was supposed to be succeeded by his namesake son, but instead it was his younger brother Richard who was crowned King Richard III in June 1483. A little over two years later, Margaret's nephew took the throne following the Battle of Bosworth as Henry VII. Henry Tudor was of course the son of King Henry's half-brother Edmund Tudor and was Margaret's nephew by marriage. He was also, however, related to her by blood. His grandmother Queen Katherine de Valois was the older sister of Margaret's uncle, King Charles VI of France. The first Tudor king was in fact a cousin of Queen Margaret on his father's side.

Shakespeare put Margaret of Anjou at the Battle of Bosworth at the conclusion of his play *Richard III*. The Bard probably knew that she died three years before the battle and was just exercising artistic licence, and it certainly worked. The battle looked like the final revenge of the shunned and wronged queen and more generally the House of Lancaster, as well as a judgement from heaven upon those who had taken the lives of Henry VI and Prince Edward. The Wars of the Roses did not really end in 1485, as there were still Yorkist claimants and at least one major battle led by one to come. Henry VII somehow managed to keep hold of his throne for twenty-four years, which is two more than Edward IV had managed. He was also the first King of England in over eighty years to be succeeded by his son. The last had been Henry V, way back in 1422. Since then, as we have seen, usurpation, murder and battle had become the methods by which new kings were selected.

Margaret never lived to see any of this happen, of course. She died in obscurity and relative poverty having lost everything and with only dogs and a few friends for companionship. Her posthumous reputation did not really improve. Henry Tudor tried at one point to get his uncle Henry VI canonised as a saint, but apparently made no attempt to redeem the name of his aunt. Of course, he barely knew Margaret personally and it is possible that he might have believed some of the rumours and propaganda about her.

One other person who was more closely related to Margaret enjoyed a happy ending, however. Katherine Vaux, her faithful friend, lady-in-waiting and companion, who had stuck by her mistress through thick and thin, returned to England after Margaret's death. Although she had lost her husband, Nicholas, at Tewkesbury, Katherine's children survived. Her son, also called Nicholas, was probably about twenty-one or twenty-two years of age when she returned home and had been growing up in the household of Lady Margaret Beaufort. Katherine had missed out on much of her children's lives, but they seem to have continued their tradition of faithful service to the Lancastrian dynasty. Nicholas junior fought at the Battle of Stoke Field on Henry Tudor's side in 1487. Katherine may also have had a daughter who married Richard Guildford, a man who was embroiled in a rebellion against Richard III in 1483. Towards the end of his own life, Nicholas junior was raised to the peerage as Baron Vaux of Harrowden in 1523. We don't know when Katherine herself died, although one source claims that she lived until 1509, and saw the coronation of King Henry VIII.

Margaret of Anjou was a woman who stepped beyond the traditional expectations of her role and defied social norms. However, if she had been successful she might have got away with it. If she had managed to restore the Lancastrian dynasty to the throne, and above all kept them there by destroying her Yorkist enemies, she might well be remembered as one of the greatest queens England ever had. She might well have be seen as an English answer to Joan of Arc. Margaret may be considered to have lost the fifteenth-century Game of Thrones that was the Wars of the Roses, but she was also on the losing side of history. The old saying that 'history is written by the victors' applies here. The Yorkists vilified Margaret, presenting her as an evil, scheming adulteress who wanted to kill her husband, marry her lover and put their dubious offspring on the throne. They did so to justify their usurpation of the throne, crafting a narrative in order to present themselves as the rightful heirs and the Lancastrian royal family as unfit to rule. It should be noted that criticisms of Henry were generally less harsh and personal, tending to be more sympathetic, albeit condescending. Chroniclers proclaimed Henry to be incompetent, but usually because he was so innocent and otherworldly. He was just too naive and easily led. He was 'a good, simple and innocent man'.

They reserved their ire for Margaret. She was the she-wolf, the vicious, aggressive and bloodthirsty despot who turned on her own family and her own country. She was unfeminine, unnatural, manipulative and cruel, ambitious, vindictive, corrupt and lacking in self-control. She was the one who slept around and taunted her enemies before stabbing them. So evil was she that she even revelled in the deaths of innocent children. In fact, Margaret in medieval and early modern depictions is so awful she is almost cartoonish. One half expects her to sprout horns and start cackling.

Yet things have not improved in the modern age. In the 2019 BBC series *The Hollow Crown*, Margaret romps in bed with the Duke of Somerset while the noble Duke of Gloucester is being murdered. It is often claimed that she was the inspiration for the notorious character of Cersei Lannister in the HBO series *Game of Thrones*, a thoroughly amoral and power-hungry woman whose offspring were the product of a lifelong incestuous affair with her twin brother. Some have even tried to draw parallels between Prince Edward of Westminster and Cersei's son Joffrey Lannister, claiming that both were the violent and sadistic products of adultery.

It is somewhat disturbing to see that the sexualised slurs directed at a fifteenth-century woman by her political adversaries still have currency today. All the more ironic are the allegations that Margaret was hungry for power and prepared to go to any lengths to get her way when the two longest-reigning monarchs in British history are women. Margaret did not do what she did because she was greedy or ambitious, but because she was protecting her family. She sought only to keep her husband on the throne and protect her son's position as his heir. When her husband was deposed, she was fighting to regain the throne for her child. Despite the vilification, despite everything, Margaret was not doing anything against the natural order of the world as fifteenth-century people conceived of it. She had married an anointed monarch and she had borne his child, who should rightly have succeeded him. She went to extreme lengths because she was forced to them, firm in her belief that what she did was justified, if at times underhanded.

Her only real 'crimes' were those against English national pride and occasionally national interests, the latter violated by her use of certain cities and towns as bargaining chips to try to gain advantage or allegiance. In the view of her contemporaries, however, Margaret's crimes were against the very order of society and politics. She violated her marriage vows and broke both God's laws and men's. She became violent and vicious, 'worse than a wolf of France'. Yet it is hard to judge Margaret for taking part in violence, or for having men executed, considering what was going on all over the country and what the men all around her were doing and had been doing for a decade – cutting down their cousins and their peers without mercy.

Margaret lost because, despite everything, she was not a commander or a military leader. She failed in the end because she had to rely on the mercy of others, and called upon the assistance of foreign mercenaries in light of her shortage of troops. She lost because the people of London refused to open the gates to her thanks to the Yorkist propaganda machine working at full tilt. Sometimes she lost due to sheer bad luck. Edward IV seemed to have the weather on his side far more often than any other king during his battles, so often that it is little wonder there were whisperings of witchcraft. Such things are what give the conflict known as the Wars of the Roses its fascinating and almost modern feel: the masterful use of propaganda, the moments of pivotal fortune, the way in which events were determined by pitched battles as opposed to sieges or long campaigns.

Perhaps Margaret's other flaw was that she was too trusting. During the period of her exile, she relied on the kindness and charity of others – her relatives, extended family and friends. All too often, she relied on financial and military support from her cousins in France, or her allies at home and abroad, and they let her down time and time again. Perhaps she was just naïve; she seems to have put too much value on familial bonds. She did not envisage the King of France, the Duke of Burgundy and others double crossing her, or reneging on their agreements. Of course, they believed that politics and alliances were more important, and they all had their own interests and agendas to serve. All too often, the interventions by these foreign players directly or indirectly influenced the outcome of events in England. It could be said that in putting so much faith in a political system based on trust and blood ties she failed to grasp how drastically politics had changed, the willingness of her fellow aristocrats and royals to go to any lengths to achieve their ends: to lie, manipulate and double cross their fellows, or to kill them.

The tragedy is that Margaret was not a *bad* queen. She was simply a woman dealt a terrible hand and confronted with unprecedented circumstances. Moreover, she was forced into a political role that she had not been prepared for and never could have been. She made the best of an awful situation and, in order to protect and advance her family's interests, did things which she knew could be used against her in future. Unlike a man or a king, however, she could not so readily get away with breaking the rules. Succeeding and winning tended to exonerate; the end justified the means. Margaret eventually resorted to fighting fire with fire, coming to believe that this was the only way to defend herself and those she loved. In the end, she lost the gamble.

Margaret died in obscurity and poverty on her father's lands, once again entirely reliant on the goodwill of others. She had been ransomed back to France because her destroyer needed money, and within a short time her executors were squabbling over her possessions. It was an ignominious end for a woman who had once claimed the regency of England and had who fought tirelessly to uphold the claims of her husband and her son.

NOTES

1 A Child of Little Account

1. Jacobus de Voragine, Christopher Stace (trans.), *The Golden Legend,* London: Penguin, 1998, pp162-5

2. *Vaughan, Richard (2002) [1970]. Philip the Good. Woodbridge, Suffolk: Boydell Press. pp. 118–9*

3. Zita Eva Rohr, *Yolande of Aragon, 1381-1442): Family and Power* (Macmillan, London, 2016), p190.1.

4. Amy Licence, *Henry VI and Margaret of Anjou, A Marriage of Unequals* (Pen and Sword, Barnsley, 2018) p50-1.

5. Alison Weir, *Lancaster and York: The Wars of the Roses* (London, 1998), p108.

6. John Watts, *Henry VI and the Politics of Kingship* (Cambridge, 1996), p91.

7. Juliet Barker, *Conquest: The English Kingdom of France in the Hundred Years War* (London, 2009), pp327-8.

2 A Royal Marriage

1. Those sent to escort Margaret to England and afterwards, to her wedding were not the same as the members of her personal retinue, which was quite small. They were more of a ceremonial thing as a one off to welcome the new Queen.
2. Watts, *Politics of Kingship,* p222.
3. Dockray, Keith. Henry VI, Margaret of Anjou and the Wars of the Roses: From Contemporary Chronicles, Letters and Records, Fonthill Media 2000, p74.
4. *Ibid*, p74.
5. Griffiths, p257-8.
6. A.R. Myers 'The Household of Margaret of Anjou: 1452-3' in Bulletin of John Rylands Library 1957; 40 (2) p82.
7. Ibid, p86.
8. Griffiths says that Boothe was not, in fact Margaret's Chancellor but rather her personal chaplain (and presumably confessor). R.A. Griffiths, The Reign of King Henry VI (Stroud, 1998), p954 n.
9. Chamberlain was another one of those ancient positions which went back centuries. Originally a Chamberlain had been a Steward or servant who looked after their master's house and household. (Hence chamber). Eventually this became the chief servant of the household and the title was just applied to high-ranking officials and nobleman. The clerk of jewels was obviously the official who looked after the Queen's jewels. Why did she need such a servant? Margaret's jewellery was probably the most valuable items that

she owned, worth many millions of pounds in today's money. She needed a trustworthy and reliable person to perform this role.

10. Lauren Johnson, *The Shadow King: The Life and Death of Henry VI* (London, 2019), p361-2.

11. Letter CXXV, in Letters of Margaret of Anjou, ed. Cecil Monro, Esq. (Camden Society, 1863), p156.

12. Letter LXXIV, p106-8.

13. Griffiths, p257-62.

14. Nancy Goldstone, *The Maid and the Queen: The Secret History of Joan of Arc* (London, 2011), p148.

15. Helen E. Maurer, *Margaret of Anjou: Queenship and Power in Later Medieval England* (Suffolk, 2003), pp25-26. Maurer notes that the actual impact of returning soldiers to local outbreaks of disorder and general lawlessness in the country may have been overstated by Chroniclers and observers.

    The general undercurrent of resentment and a belief that the government had failed in their duty to protect England's possessions in France and protect the interests of its people contributed to this.

16. Helen Matthews, *The Legitimacy of Bastards* (Pen and Sword Books, 2019), p216.

17. Lauren Johnson, *The Shadow King, Henry VI*, p248.

18. Maurer, p35-6.

19. Joanna Laynesmith, *The Last Medieval Queens, English Queenship 1445-1503* (Cambridge, 2004) p185.

20. Three fifteenth-century chronicles, with historical memoranda by John Stowe, the antiquary, and

contemporary notes of occurrences written by him in the reign of Queen Elizabeth edited by James Gairdner, London, 1845 p94-100.

21. *Ibid*, p255.

22. Elizabeth Hallam, ed, Chronicles of the Wars of the Roses, (London, 1988), p205.

23. Helen Maurer and B.M. Chron ed. *The Letters of Margaret of Anjou* (Boydell and Brewer, 2019), p47-8.

24. Hallam, p206,

25. The Chronicles of England and France in Two Parts by Robert Fabyan, ed. Henry Ellis (London, 1841), p635, 653-4.

26. Lauren Johnson, The Shadow King, p273.

27. Ibid, p206.

28. Dockray, p125.

29. Ibid.

30. Ibid, p93-4

31. C.M. Woolgar, *The Great Household in Late Medieval England* (Yale University Press, 1999), p10, p161.

32. Dockray, p93-4.

33. Michael Hicks, *Wars of the Roses* (Yale University Press 2010), p49-51.

34. Ibid, p122. 1452 was of presumably a leap year.

35. Dockray, p122.

3 The French Queen

1. Weir, p172.

2. Johnson, p293.

3. Laynesmith, Last Medieval Queens, p138.

4. R.A. Griffiths, The Reign of King Henry VI (Stroud, 1998), p256.

5. Weir, p171-2

6. A.J. Pollard, *John Talbot and the War in France, 1427-1453*, (Pen and Sword, Barnsley, 2005) p136.

7. Ibid, p138.

8. Hallam, p212.

9. Johnson, p312.

10. Watts, p306-7.

11. Johnson, p309.

12. Griffiths, p722.

13. Dockray, p138.

14. Ibid, P723.

15. Maurer, p108.

16. Ibid, p109.

17. Ibid, p113-14.

18. Johnson, p319.

19. Hallam, p214

20. PR 1455, Item 19. Given-Wilson, Chris, Brand, Paul, Phillips, Seymour, Ormrod, Mark, Martin, Geoffrey, Curry, Anne and Horrox, Rosemary, eds. Parliament Rolls of Medieval England Woodbridge: 2005, British History Online, http://www.british-history.ac.uk/no-series/parliament-rolls-medieval accessed 21st July 2021.

21. Margaret L. Kekewich, Colin Richmond, John Watts, Anne F. Sutton, Lisser Visser-Fuchs, eds. *The Politics of Fifteenth Century England: John Vale's Book* (Sutton, 1995), p191.

22. Dockray, p144.

23. Dockray, p145.

24. Dockray, p146.

25. Ibid.

26. Helen Maurer and B. M. Cron, ed. *The Letters of Margaret of Anjou* (Boydell and Brewer, 2019), p164-5.

27. The letter is contained in BL, Add. MS 46,846, fol. 55v; and also appears transcribed on p164 of *The Letters of Margaret of Anjou*. The hunting lodge and park at Ware were owned by the Earl of Salisbury at this time. The possibility that York's father-in-law may have invited Margaret to his park for some time to indulge in one of her favourite pastimes at this fraught time is interesting.

4 The She Wolf

1. Michael Hicks, *The Wars of the Roses*, p124-5.

2. *Ibid.*

3. Griffiths, p782. The formal and eloquent way in which a child who was barely more than three or four years of age referred to his mother may seem surprising, but it is likely these were not his actual words. They were in fact a standard mode of address used in formal documents which were likely signed off for the prince.

4. Ibid, p782-3.

5. Ibid.

6. Amy Licence, *Henry VI and Margaret of Anjou: A Marriage of Unequals* (Pen and Sword, Barnsley, 2018), p140.

7. Grufydd had two sons who served alongside Jasper Tudor, and his grandson, Sir Rhys at Thomas, was an important supporter of Henry Tudor. Rhys was referred to as 'the man who killed Richard III' for the pivotal role that he is said to have played in the Battle of Bosworth, being one of the men who supposedly struck the fatal blows which killed the King. It appears then that Margaret's attempts to ensure the family remained staunch Lancastrians were more successful than she could ever had hoped.

8. Maurer, p140.

9. Hicks, p125-6.

10. Griffiths, p785.

11. Dockray, p154. Also, Johnson, p351.

12. Johnson, Ibid.

13. Hall's English Chronicle ed. Grafton, Richard, J. (London, 1809), p235.

14. Hicks, p134.

15. Dockray, p154.

16. Maurer, p152.

5 The Beginning of Sorrows

1. Licence, p146.

2. Johnson, p367.

3. Dockray, p151.

4. Dockray, p152.

5. Other sources suggest he had as few as 3000 men, although one inflates the figure up to 8000.

6. Dan Spencer, *The Castle in the Wars of the Roses* (Pen and Sword, 2020), p42.

7. Johnson, p375.
8. Partial text of the Somniem Vigilantis can be found in Dockray, p98. See also, J.H. Flemming, ed. *England Under the Lancastrians* (London, 1921). p143-5. Michael Hicks also made a good modern translation in 2013.
9. Maurer, p173.
10. Susan Higginbotham, *The Prince who did not become King: Edward of Lancaster, 1453-1471* (Self-Published, Susan Higginbotham, 2011), p7-8.
11. Dockray, p160.
12. Licence, p380.
13. Johnson, p386.

6 Queen Rampant

1. Bertram Wolfe, Henry VI (Yale University Press, 1983), p323.
2. Maurer, p176.
3. Dockray, p166.
4. *Ibid*, p163-4
5. Bertram Wolfe, *Henry VI* (Yale University Press, 1983), p325.
6. Hicks, *Wars of the Roses*, p158.
7. Maurer, p188-9.
8. Johnson, p409.
9. Hicks, p160.
10. Licence, p175.
11. Dockray, p178.
12. Clement Paston to John Paston I, 23rd January 1461, in Norman Davis ed. *The Paston Letters* (Oxford, 1963), p62-3.

13. B. M. Cron, 'Margaret of Anjou and the Lancastrian March on London, 1461', *The Ricardian,* Vol. 11 No 147. December 1999, p607-8.
14. Johnson, p413.
15. Ibid, p419.
16. Chron, 'Margaret of Anjou and the Lancastrian March on London, p604
17. Licence, p181.
18. Weir, p273.
19. Dockray, p183-4.

7 Queen in Exile

1. Maurer and Chron, *Letters of Margaret of Anjou,* p236-7.
2. John Neville was, as his surname suggests, a member of the same family from whom Richard Neville Earl of Warwick sprang. John was a first cousin of Warwick, as both men were grandsons of Richard Neville Earl of Westmoreland. However, there had arisen a bitter feud between two of the branches of the Neville family as a result of Westmoreland having been married twice and favouring the children by his second marriage.
3. This story is so widespread that the author heard it recounted at Leeds Royal Armouries in 2019. It is generally believed that Clifford was wearing a hinged bevor, a piece of plate armour that covered the collarbone, neck and lower part of the throat. By the 15th century it was sometimes made in two pieces and fitted with a hinge, the upper part could be lowered away from the mouth, giving the wearer more room to breathe. Clifford had lowered his bevor, to

breathe or perhaps speak more easily, and was alleged to have been hit by an arrow, but presumably in the mouth or larynx rather that the lower part of the throat.

4. Licence, p185.
5. Anthony Goodman, *The Wars of the Roses: The Soldier's Experience* (Stroud, 2006), p191.
6. Wolfe, p333.
7. Johnson, p435.
8. *Ibid.*
9. Maurer and Chron, *Letters of Margaret of Anjou*, p242-6.
10. Wolfe, p334.
11. Johnson, p449-50
12. Ibid.
13. Spencer, *The Castle in the Wars of the Roses*, p86-7
14. Johnson, p453.

8 The Wheel of Fortune

1. Licence, p201-2.
2. Goodman, p200-201.
3. Johnson, p461.
4. Dockray, p204.
5. Licence, p207-8, Johnson, p468-9.
6. Dockray, p204, Licence, Ibid.
7. Letters of Margaret of Anjou, p271-3.
8. Dockray, p206.

9 Victory and Death

1. Johnson, p496
2. Wolfe, p345.

3. Weir, p378-9.
4. John Gillingham, *The Wars of the Roses: Peace and Conflict in 15th Century England* (Phoenix Press, 1981), p221
5. Weir, Ibid.
6. Dockray. P211.
7. *Ibid*, p214.
8. Licence, p226.

10 Once Called Queen

1. Dockray, p208.
2. Johnson, p516.
3. Licence, p233.
4. Johnson, Op Cit, p516-17.
5. Licence, p234. See also J. Huizinga, *The Waning of the Middle Ages* (London, 1924), p300.

BIBLIOGRAPHY

Primary Sources

Christine de Pizan, Rosalind Brown Grant, trans. *The Book of the City of the Ladies* (London, 1999).

Christine de Pizan, Sarah Lawson, trans. *The Treasure of the City of the Ladies* (London, 1985).

Hall's English Chronicle ed. Grafton, Richard, J. (London, 1809).

The Chronicles of England and France in Two Parts by Robert Fabyan, ed. Ellis, Henry (London, 1841).

Jacobus de Voragine, Richard Hamer, ed. Christoper Stace, trans. *The Golden Legend* (London, 1988).

Kekewich, Margaret L., Colin Richmond, John Watts, Anne F. Sutton, Lisser Visser-Fuchs, eds. *The Politics of Fifteenth Century England: John Vale's Book* (Sutton, 1995).

Letters of Margaret of Anjou, ed. Cecil Monro, Esq. (Camden Society, 1863).

Maurer, Helen and Chron, B.M. ed. *The Letters of Margaret of Anjou* (Boydell and Brewer, 2019),

Given-Wilson, Chris, Brand, Paul, Phillips, Seymour, Ormrod, Mark, Martin, Geoffrey, Curry, Anne and Horrox, Rosemary, eds. Parliament Rolls of Medieval England Woodbridge: 2005, British History Online.

Three fifteenth-century chronicles, with historical memoranda by John Stowe, the antiquary, and contemporary notes of occurrences written by him in the reign of Queen Elizabeth edited by James Gairdner (London, 1854).

Secondary Sources

Barker, Juliet, *Conquest: The English Kingdom of France in the Hundred Years War* (London, 2009).

Castor, *Helen, Joan of Arc: A History* (London, 2014).

Chron, B.M., 'Margaret of Anjou and the Lancastrian March on London, 1461', *The Ricardian,* Vol. 11 No 147. December 1999.

Dockray, Keith, *Henry VI, Margaret of Anjou and the Wars of the Roses: From Contemporary Chronicles, Letters and Records* (Fonthill Media 2000).

Flemming J.H., ed. *England Under the Lancastrians* (London, 1921).

Gillingham, John, *The Wars of the Roses: Peace and Conflict in fifteenth century England* (Phoenix Press, 1981).

Goodman, Anthony, *The Wars of the Roses: The Soldier's Experience* (Stroud, 2006).

Goldstone, Nancy, *The Maid and the Queen: The Secret History of Joan of Arc* (London, 2011).

Griffiths, R.A., The Reign of King Henry VI (Stroud, 1998).

Hallam, Elizabeth, ed. *Chronicles of the Wars of the Roses* (London, 1988).

Hicks, Michael, *Wars of the Roses* (Yale University Press, 2010).

Higginbotham, Susan, *The Prince who did not become King: Edward of Lancaster, 1453-1471* (Self-Published, Susan Higginbotham, 2011).

Huizinga, J., *The Waning of the Middle Ages* (London, 1924).

Kekewich, Margaret, *The Good King, René of Anjou and Fifteenth Century Europe* (Macmillan, 2008).

Johnson, Lauren, *The Shadow King: The Life and Death of Henry VI* (London, 2019).

Laynesmith, Joanna, *The Last Medieval Queens, English Queenship 1445-1503* (Cambridge, 2004).

Licence, Amy, *Henry VI and Margaret of Anjou: A Marriage of Unequals* (Barnsley, 2018).

Matthews, Helen, *The Legitimacy of Bastards* (Pen and Sword Books, 2019).

Maurer, Helen E., *Margaret of Anjou: Queenship and Power in Later Medieval England* (Suffolk, 2003).

Myers. A.R., 'The Household of Margaret of Anjou: 1452-3' in Bulletin of John Rylands Library 1957; 40 (2).

Pollard, A.J., *John Talbot and the War in France, 1427-1453* (Barnsley, 2005).

Rohr, Zita Eva, *Yolande of Aragon, 1381-1442: Family and Power* (London, 2016).

Ross, James, *Henry VI: A Good, Simple and Innocent Man* (London, 2019).

Spencer, Dan, *The Castle in the Wars of the Roses* (Pen and Sword, 2020),

Vaughan, Richard, *Philip the Good* (Suffolk, 2002).

Watts, John, *Henry VI and the Politics of Kingship* (Cambridge, 1996).

Weir, Alison, *Lancaster, and York: The Wars of the Roses* (London, 1998).

Wolfe, Bertram, *Henry VI* (Yale University Press, 1983).

Woolgar, C.M., *The Great Household in Late Medieval England* (Yale University Press, 1999).

ACKNOWLEDGEMENTS

Thanks to my family members, who tolerated me closeting myself away for hours to write this book. Especially to my mother and Vickki who proofread this book in manuscript form.

Thanks to Shaun Barrington at Amberley Publishing for extending my deadline due to Covid (which sadly meant that I could not travel to France to visit any of the places associated with Margaret).

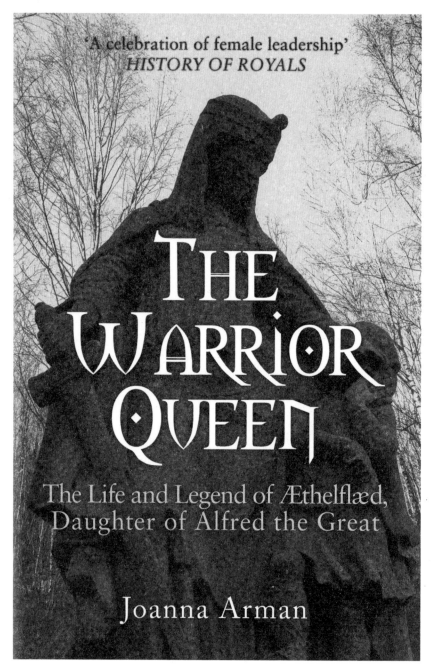

Also available from Amberley Publishing

From the author of *Richard, Duke of York*:
'A much-needed biography' DAN JONES

THE
WARS
OF THE
ROSES

The Key Players in
the Struggle for
Supremacy

MATTHEW LEWIS

Available from all good bookshops or to order direct
Please call **01453-847-800**
www.amberley-books.com

Also available from Amberley Publishing

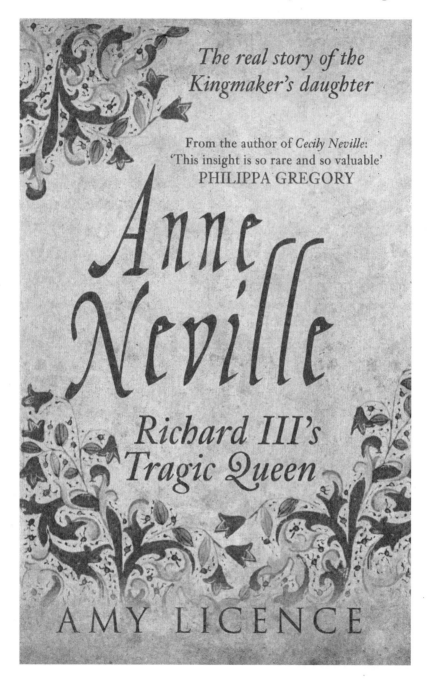

The real story of the
Kingmaker's daughter

From the author of *Cecily Neville*:
'This insight is so rare and so valuable'
PHILIPPA GREGORY

Anne Neville

Richard III's Tragic Queen

AMY LICENCE

Also available from Amberley Publishing

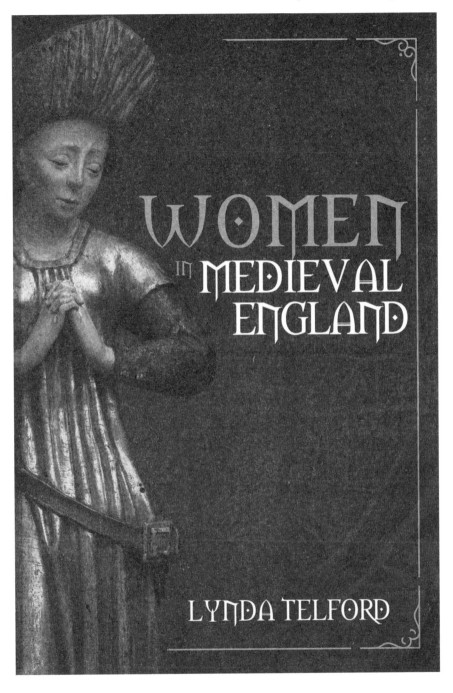

WOMEN IN MEDIEVAL ENGLAND

LYNDA TELFORD

Also available from Amberley Publishing

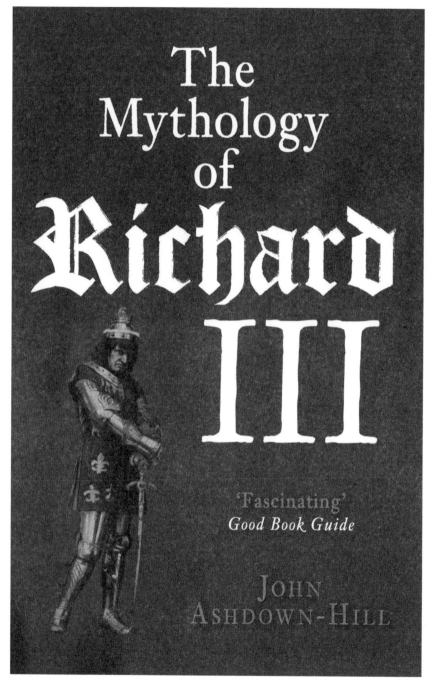

The
Mythology
of
Richard
III

'Fascinating'
Good Book Guide

JOHN
ASHDOWN-HILL

Available from all good bookshops or to order direct
Please call **01453-847-800**
www.amberley-books.com